# WHICH NATIVE FOREST PLANT?

A Simple Guide to the Identification, Ecology and Uses of New Zealand's Native Forest Shrubs, Climbers, Perching Plants & Groundcovers

# ANDREW CROWE

T0362795

PENGUIN BOOKS

# Introduction to Ecology Edition

The original *Which?* books were designed to do two things: to make plant identification simple and include a wide range of traditional Māori and European uses of the plants – the human story. This new edition extends this approach by adding details of the origins of Māori and English common names and attempts to go beyond this rather people-centred view of nature to portray the bigger picture of nature's interconnectedness – that is, how the whole jigsaw of the forest fits together.

**BIRDS, LIZARDS AND BATS** The pieces of this jigsaw fit more tightly together than most people realise, for many native birds depend on specific native plants for nectar or fruit or as a source of nesting material; the same is true of lizards, bats and insects, many of which feed on the nectar. In return, many of these creatures provide some kind of service to the plant: pollination in the case of nectar feeders or, in the case of those feeding on the fruit, transport of seeds. Over millions of years this interdependent relationship has come to a kind of balance in which all parties continue to survive. The challenge of our time is that the forest is not so well adapted to the newcomers: e.g. people, possums, pigs, deer, goats, rats, mice and wasps.

**INSECTS AND MITES** Many New Zealand native plants have at least one kind of insect that depends some stage in its life-cycle on that plant for its food. Many of these creatures are active only at night and are seldom seen, but their presence is often evident from chew marks on the leaves, for example. Torn leaves are a likely indication of possum damage; nibble marks and holes are often the result of feeding insects (such as beetles, or the caterpillars of moths); pale squiggly lines inside leaves are a tell-tale sign of tunnelling maggots of a 'leafminer fly' or tiny caterpillars of a specialist 'leafminer moth'. Other invertebrates will leave distinctive lumps ('galls') on the plant. Indeed, there are so many kinds of plant-feeding insects that it is not possible to mention all. The aim here is rather to provide a simple guide to the more conspicuous or distinctive ones.

**FLOWER COLOURS** There is an almost complete lack of large or colourful flowers in the New Zealand forest, with bright reds, blues and purples almost entirely absent. This peculiarity of the flora is linked to the colour perception of different local pollinators, most of which are insects. Significantly, New Zealand has few butterflies, more than twice the number of fly species of comparable countries, a third the number of wasps and bees, and no native long-tongued bees.

> **Blue** and **purple** flowers generally attract butterflies and introduced bees.

> **Red** flowers in the New Zealand native flora are either large and adapted for bird pollination, or small and adapted for visits by flies and native bees.

> **Yellow** flowers are generally good at drawing flies, native bees and beetles.

> **White** is the colour of most New Zealand native flowers; these flowers are often tiny, conspicuous only by being crowded together. By day, this suits the flies. At night, white catches the moonlight, attracting the attention of moths – especially if the flower is scented.

> **Green** flowers are also common in New Zealand. Many of these are small and scented, making them attractive to flies in particular.

## PHOTOS
Wherever possible, images in the margins are shown life-size. (For reasons of space, illustrations of bats and birds are reduced.) Captions identifying these images appear as red type in the text.

# Using this Book

he concept behind this book is to help trampers and day-trippers get to know the plants that
e most often noticed along tracksides through native forest. Where tracks go through scrub
regenerating forest, it should work equally well.

## shrub, climber, perching plant or groundcover?

**hrubs** are woody plants with no central trunk. (**Trees** usually have a trunk.)
**limbers** are plants whose stems climb up other plants.
**erching plants** are plants that specialise in perching in the forks of trees.
**roundcovers** are smaller and generally have no woody stem.
**rees** are covered in *Which Native Tree?* and **ferns** in *Which Native Fern?*)

---

### What kind of leaf?

There are basically four ways in which leaves (or leaflets*) can be arranged
on a branch or stalk: in tufts, hand-shaped, alternating, or opposite.

| In tufts | Hand-shaped (with 3 or more fingers) | Alternating | Opposite (all in pairs) |
|---|---|---|---|

Some leaves have teeth along the edges; others have none; and some are lobed.

| Teeth | No teeth | Lobed |
|---|---|---|

---

be precise, plants have either 'simple' leaves or 'compound' ones made up of individual 'leaflets'. But the layperson (and this book)
erally refers to both leaves and leaflets simply as 'leaves'. Later, as you get to know more about plants, it will help to know the
erence between a simple leaf and a group of leaflets that makes a compound leaf. Leaf buds are the clue. If it has a bud at its base,
n it is a leaf and not a leaflet. (Examples of plants in this book with compound leaves are maukoro, puawānanga, tātarāmoa and piripiri.)

## Using the leaf keys

1. Find a typical leaf of a common trackside plant. Don't pull it off because later you'll need look at how it grows on the plant. Now turn to page 5 and decide which type of leaf it is. The turn to the page indicated.

2. Starting from the arrow at the bottom of this new page, follow the appropriate branches un you arrive at an illustration of your leaf. Now turn to the page indicated for a close-u photograph of that leaf.

3. Just to be sure, run down the checklist next to the photograph, giving special attention text in italics.

If you have any trouble matching your leaf to the key or run into any problems, turn to Troubleshooting on page 62.

## Using the plant pages

Plants that look similar are paired to appear on facing pages. Use the identification checklist on these pages to distinguish between them. The following graphics show the approximat distribution and common size of each plant.

A guide to the approximate geographic range within which the wild plant is usually found.

The common shape and height of the mature plant with an adult person or a copy of this book next to it to give scale.

A guide to the altitudes where the plant naturally grows (in metres).

700m

## Another approach: the flowers and berries key

Because it is often the flowers or berries of a plant that first catch one's eye, there is also a ke to these. Turn to page 61. What colour is the flower or fruit? Follow that coloured band up th diagram until you arrive at the appropriate flower or fruit. Turn to the page indicated and use th checklist on that page.

## Māori names

Names (whether Māori or not) vary from region to region. For simplicity, the commonest are used but others are included and are just as valid. The correct pronunciation of Māori vowels is a follows: 'a' as in 'far', 'e' as in 'bet', 'i' as in 'me', 'o' as in 'or', 'u' as in 'flu'. To help with pronunciation the macrons have been included; these indicate a lengthened vowel, e.g. ā = aa.

## Nature notes

The study of ecology involves patient observation. With so much still to be learnt in this field the observant reader (young or old) has a good chance of making new discoveries – especiall with the aid of a camera and good record-keeping. (See pages 2 and 63 for more on fores ecology.)

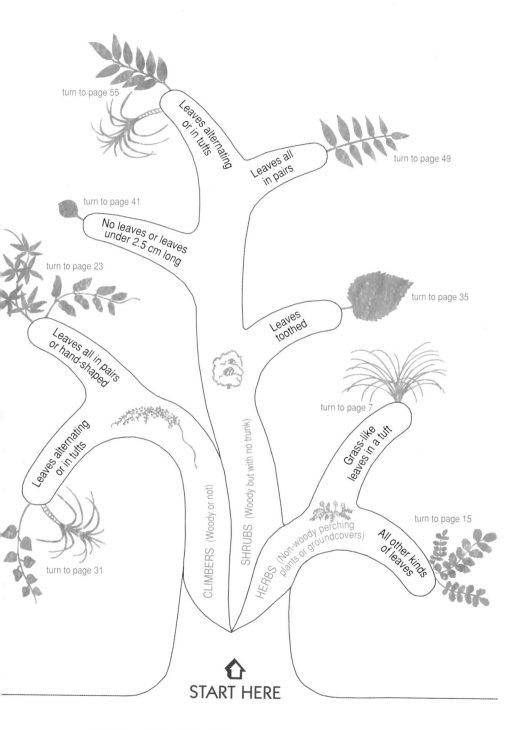

turn to page 55

Leaves alternating or in tufts

Leaves all in pairs

turn to page 49

turn to page 41

No leaves or leaves under 2.5 cm long

turn to page 23

turn to page 35

Leaves all in pairs or hand-shaped

Leaves toothed

Leaves alternating or in tufts

turn to page 7

CLIMBERS (Woody or not)

SHRUBS (Woody but with no trunk)

Grass-like leaves in a tuft

turn to page 15

turn to page 31

HERBS (Non-woody perching plants or groundcovers)

All other kinds of leaves

START HERE

YOU CAN MEASURE YOUR LEAF HERE ├── 2.5 cm ──┤

**5**

# Māpere
# Cutty Grass

*Gahnia setifolia* [Family: Cyperaceae]

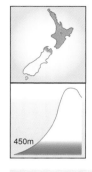

450m

| | |
|---|---|
| **Leaves:** | *Long, harsh and cutting*, growing in a tuft |
| **Flowers:** | Tall, weeping flower heads on a solid, triangular stem (spring) |
| **Seeds:** | Reddish-brown; can hang on the plant for up to two years |
| **Other:** | Common in light forest and scrub |

The stems were used by Māori as play spears; māpere means to throw or flick. Other Māori names, **toetoe tarangārara** and **toetoe ngaungau** refer to the stinging cuts the plant inflicts when one brushes against it. Hence also the name, cutty grass. To appreciate the plant's weaponry, take a look at a leaf through a magnifying glass. At least a dozen rows of saw-like teeth are laid out along either side of the leaf's centre line, each row having 8–12 teeth per centimetre. With a little calculation it is clear how when just 10 centimetres of leaf rubs against you, some 2000 teeth find a chance to hook into your skin. Related sedges in Australia are known as 'saw edge' plants. New Zealand has many other grass-like plants with cutting leaves that are also popularly known as cutty grass: native toetoe and its introduced cousin, pampas grass (neither of them generally common in native forest), as well as all the *Carex* sedges and even hook grass. In spite of its common name, this plant is not really a grass, but actually a type of sedge (distinguished from true grasses by the solid triangular cross-section of its stem). The tall, slightly nodding, seed heads carry small, dark brown to reddish-brown seeds that swing from the flower stalks by long threads – a feature that clearly distinguishes it from the more familiar toetoe grass or pampas. Māori also used the leaves for thatching.

**Nature Notes:** On Codfish Island (and previously on Little Barrier Island), kākāpō (top right) eat the juicy portion of *Gahnia* leaves. Kiwi will sometimes sleep beneath plants during the day; hence an alternative name for the plant, **toetoe kiwi**. Two kinds of 'ridge-backed stick insects' and the 'forest shield bug' feed on the leaves. Native caterpillars that feed on it include those of the 'forest ringlet butterfly', 'pale wainscot' moth (*Tmetolophota arotis*), and sedge moth (*Proditrix gahniae*, which feed inside the new shoot). Grubs of several species of beetle feed inside the leaves and bases of stems, while a 'cutty grass seed bug' (*Margareta dominica*) sucks the seeds. Living in the seedheads and among the leaves is the 'cutty grass mealybug'. Goats generally leave the plants alone.

**Growing It:** Difficult to cultivate and not generally used in cultivation.

**Māpere / Cutty Grass**
*(leaves cutting)*
page 6

&

**Mīkoikoi / New Zealand Iris**
*(leaves smooth)*
page 14

Leaves mostly
5–8 mm wide

**Tūrutu / Blueberry**
*(leaves folded in a fan)*
page 13

&

**Bush Rice Grass**
*(leaves ribbed underneath)*
page 12

Leaves mostly
8–20 mm wide

PERCHING
LILIES:
**Kahakaha**
*(leaf bases black)*
page 11

&

**Kōwharawhara**
*(leaf bases not black)*
page 10

Leaves over
20 mm wide

**Kamu / Hook Grass**
*(seeds hooked)*
page 9

&

**Carex Bush Sedge**
*(seeds not hooked)*
page 8

Leaves under
5 mm wide

⬆
CONTINUE HERE

YOU CAN MEASURE THE WIDTH OF YOUR LEAF HERE    0  5  8        20 mm

# Carex Bush Sedge

*Carex dissita* [Family: Cyperaceae]

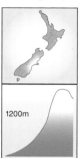

1200m

| | |
|---|---|
| **Leaves:** | M-shaped cross-section. *Often reddish or orange-green with bright red edges* |
| **Seeds:** | *The dark spiky seed clusters look rather like miniature pine cones; the seeds themselves carry no hooks (summer)* |
| **Other:** | Grows in a tuft. Bare of seedheads, it can easily be confused with hook grass (opposite) |

Very common along forest tracksides, scrub and swampy ground, particularly along the edges of forest ponds and streams. Like all sedges, the flower stem is three-angled and solid. Its seeds are borne on long, loose stems, which eventually droop to the ground to deposit the seeds some distance from the plant. The Māori name **pūrei** (recorded for 'Carex diandra and perhaps other species') is likely to have applied to this common species too; it means 'patch or cluster'. Like many other sedges, this one has rough edges to its leaves, the roughness being due to hundreds of tiny, razor-sharp teeth that can easily be seen through a magnifying glass. As with the leaves of the larger cutty grass (*Gahnia*), these can easily inflict a deep and painful wound to the unwary passer-by. Indeed, the word *Carex* means cutting; while *dissita* means spaced, referring to the wide spacing between the seed clusters. There are between 1500 and 2000 species of *Carex* in the world, over 70 of which are found in New Zealand. Of these, 61 are found in no other country.

**Nature Notes:** Kākāpō on Stewart Island have been observed chewing the leaf tips and, on Little Barrier Island, leaf remains have been found in their droppings. The plants are also eaten by takahē. Ground birds frequently use the plants for shelter and nesting. Several forest birds such as tīeke (saddlebacks) also collect the leaves as nesting material. As for insect life, the caterpillars of 'dark underwing wainscot' moths feed on the leaves. *Carex* plants in general support several species of native 'sedge weevils', 'sedge longhorn beetles' and 'sedge caterpillars', most of which tunnel into the stalks of the plant or feed on the leaves. Plants are not generally eaten by goats.

**Growing It:** Though this particular species is not widely used in cultivation, *Carex* sedges in general can be easily grown from seed or more commonly by division. Several native *Carex* sedges with interesting leaf colours are grown as ornamental plants – both in New Zealand and overseas. (Note that some introduced *Carex* species can also be a nuisance.)

# Kamu
# Hook Grass

*Carex uncinata* [Family: Cyperaceae]

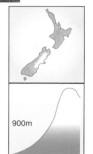

900m

**Leaves:** Narrow, grass-like and rather rough to touch

**Seeds:** *Hooked, with fish-hook-like barbs*, on straight stalks (summer)

**Other:** Forming tufts up to 50 cm high, in forest and scrub

'Kamu' means 'snare'. Widely known as hook grass, although the common name should technically be 'hooked sedge', for kamu is not a grass at all, but a sedge (distinguished from a true grass by the solid triangular section of its stem). An alternative Māori name tells more of a story: **matau-a-Māui** (the 'hook of Māui'). This refers to the fabled Māui learning from his mother about the effectiveness of a barbed hook for bird spearing. The hook referred to in all these names is a tiny fish-hook extension of the seed. This is the feature that most often brings the plant to the attention of trampers, for these hooks frequently attach themselves in huge numbers to any hairy leg or piece of clothing that happens to brush against them. This hitch-hiking approach to seed distribution may seem surprising in a country that has no native furry animals, but these seeds are known to ride on the feathers of native ground birds such as kiwi. Such a method of transporting its seeds long distances is especially important for *Uncinia* sedges, since many members of the group grow only in high-altitude areas separated from each other by low country inhospitable to them. This tactic of catching a ride allows seeds from isolated plant populations to effectively colonise and recolonise ecologically isolated areas.

**Nature Notes:** Kākāriki (top middle) eat the seeds. Originally, the hooked seeds were spread primarily by kiwi, weka (top left) and other ground birds, but trampers' socks and hairy human legs now help. Several species of birds (including tomtit and fantail) get entangled and are occasionally trapped by the plants. Leaves are eaten by takahē and, on Codfish Island, by kākāpō. Also supports caterpillars of the 'white-line owlet' moth (*Graphania infensa*), the grubs of at least two 'sedge longhorn beetles', several 'sedge weevils' and several 'sedge fungus weevils'. Generally left alone, though, by farm animals, wild pigs, goats and deer.

**Growing It:** Though not generally cultivated, a form with bright reddish-brown leaves has been advertised – for decorative and groundcover use – as the 'copperware shrub'.

GROUNDCOVERS

**9**

# Kōwharawhara
# Perching Lily

*Astelia solandri* [Family: Asteliaceae]

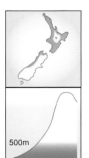

500m

| Leaves: | Tufted, grass-like, 1–2 m long, narrow, *silvery beneath, with three deep grooves* |
|---|---|
| **Flowers:** | Yellowish-white, on spreading fingers, sweetly scented (most of the year) |
| **Fruit:** | Small, round, translucent green to yellow or dull brown (most of the year) |
| **Other:** | *Growing mostly in trees, but sometimes on the ground* |

The Māori name links this plant with the ground-growing **coastal astelia** (*Astelia banksii*), likening their leaf fibre to that of the hara (*Pandanus*) of the tropical Pacific. Of 13 species of native *Astelia*, kōwharawhara is the only one that commonly perches – forming huge, flax-like clumps on the limbs and trunks of forest trees (though also found within wet forest on rocks). The small, ripe fruits were eaten by Māori and the snow-white downy fibres from the underside of the leaves used by women as decorative hair ties. Leaves were also worn by girls as headbands. The oil from the small seeds is high in *γ-linolenic acid* (GLA), an essential fatty acid required by the body, small amounts of which are believed to be effective in treating pre-menstrual syndrome, multiple sclerosis and diabetes. Of the ground-growing astelias, probably the best known is **kauri grass** (*A. trinervia*) which, as its common name suggests, is common in the undergrowth of kauri forest.

**Nature Notes:** In summer, large clusters of creamy white flowers attract stitchbirds, bees (native and introduced) and large flies. Berries are eaten by kererū, possums and ship rats. Saddlebacks gather leaf fibre for nest-building, while ruru (moreporks), falcons, kōkako and even grey ducks have all been found nesting in the plants themselves, alongside tree-climbing 'kauri snails', Archey's frogs, giant native 'leaf-veined slugs' and two species of 'ridge-backed stick insects'. Possums will also make their dens up here. Specialist invertebrates here include the caterpillars of the 'orange Astelia wainscot' moth (top) and 'buff-tipped lily moth' (*Proditrix tetragona*, right), two 'astelia flat mites', a 'native-lily mealybug' and an 'asteliad leafminer weevil'. Ground plants are eaten by goats and deer.

**Growing It:** Propagated by seed from ripe fruit. Large clumps can be divided. Although primarily a perching plant, it flourishes on the ground too and can be used as a container plant. It looks best, however, when attached to the trunk or fork of a tree (with moss around its roots to keep them moist). Otherwise requires a friable and well-drained soil.

# Kahakaha
# Perching Lily
*Astelia hastata* [Family: Asteliaceae]

**Leaves:** Tufted, grass-like, 60–170 cm long, *broad, with black leaf bases, arranged in fans*

**Flowers:** Green, on spreading fingers, faintly scented (late summer)

**Fruit:** Turning red (autumn and winter)

**Other:** *Growing in trees, on rocks, or on the ground*

Māori used the leaves for making snow sandals; the plant's name likens its leaf-fibre to the strong coconut fibre (kaha) of the tropical Pacific. The ripe crimson fruit tastes sweet and juicy and was also no doubt eaten. These lilies perch in the forks of forest trees, their moist surfaces providing a platform for many other plants to perch. Often, the accumulated weight of the clump will eventually send it falling to the forest floor where the plant continues to grow. When kauri trees were still being felled, trees were renowned for dropping these enormously heavy loads (this species and the one on the facing page), inspiring the memorable bushman's nickname for them, '**widow-makers**'.

**Nature Notes:** Analysis of the fur, stomach and guano of short-tailed bats indicates that they visit the flowers and feed on the fruit. The fruit is also eaten by ship rats and possums. Kōkako strip fibre from dead leaves and take leaf-bases for their nests. Plants are used as nest sites by possums, Archey's frogs and birds such as New Zealand falcons. The ridged leaves channel rainwater into a reservoir in the plant's leafy, funnel-shaped base. In dry weather, some of the plant's roots tap into this stored moisture, absorbing nutrients from the rotting leaf remains collected there. Intriguingly, this reservoir (at least in the Auckland region) also provides a home to the kahakaha mosquito' (*Culex asteliae*) whose wrigglers develop in this stored water. Similar perching, water-reservoir plants from tropical America even provide sufficient water for the development of frogs. Specialist insects supported by the plant include the caterpillars of the 'orange Astelia wainscot' moth and 'buff-tipped lily moth' (*Proditrix tetragona*) – both illustrated on page 10, a 'native-lily longhorn' beetle, two 'kahakaha weevils' (including a 'kahakaha leafminer weevil', *Phorostichus linearis*), and two 'asteliad weevils' (including an 'asteliad leafminer weevil').

**Growing It:** With moss packed around the roots to retain moisture, young plants can be attached to the fork of a tree. As in nature they will grow on the ground too, preferring a well-drained soil. Though tolerating full sun, they look their best in shade. With male and female flowers on separate plants, both sexes will need to be planted to obtain fruit.

# Bush Rice Grass

*Microlaena avenacea* [Family: Poaceae]

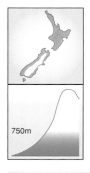

750m

| Leaves: | Blue-green on top; broad, rasping along the edges; and flat, with obvious midribs below |
|---|---|
| Seeds: | Tall, slender, arching, feathery seedheads up to 60 cm long (early summer) |
| Other: | Grows in a smallish tuft in damp, shady places within native forest |

With common names like bush rice grass and **forest rice grass**, it might come as a surprise that the botanical name *avenacea* likens the plant to an oat grass. On one point, the names agree: this is one of the few true grasses of New Zealand native forest. As more sensitive plants of the forest floor disappear, this plant's resistance to browsing by goats and deer and trampling by people has led to it becoming common, particularly along tracksides; few areas of lowland forest are now without it. The plant is, however, eaten by horses and cattle and when other grasses in marginal farmland were in short supply, its generous tuft of coarse leaves proved useful. Indeed the plant was recommended by Thomas Kirk in 1876, as being one of the few grasses well adapted for sowing in forests where cattle had access. Nowadays though, with so little native forest healthily regenerating, it would be better to fence such patches of remnant forest on farms to exclude stock altogether. (Farmers wishing to do this may consider contacting their local branch of the Queen Elizabeth II National Trust regarding covenanting such land for long-term protection.)

**Nature Notes:** Provides shelter and nesting sites for ground birds and (on the Coromandel Peninsula) daytime retreats for Archey's frogs. Plants are not generally eaten by goats or deer, but pigs eat the leaves and seeds, as do horse and cattle (see above). Caterpillars found on the plants are likely to be those of a 'white-line owlet' moth (*Graphania infensa*) or the similar-looking 'dark underwing wainscot' moth (*Tmetolophota sulcana*). Leaves are also mined by the tiny caterpillars of the widespread 'grass miner moth' (*Elachista*). The plant also supports a couple of species of native mealybug.

**Growing It:** Not widely grown but useful as an attractive shade-tolerant grass. Prefers a moist soil and looks its best as a groundcover beneath the shade of trees. Easy to grow from seed or by division.

# Tūrutu
# Blueberry

*Dianella nigra* [Family: Xanthorrhoeaceae]

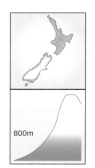

800m

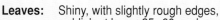

**Leaves:** Shiny, with slightly rough edges, reddish at base, 25–60 cm long, *arranged mostly in fans very much like a miniature New Zealand flax*

**Flowers:** Whitish, but rather inconspicuous (late spring)

**Fruit:** From very *pale blue-grey to deep blue or purple* (summer)

summer, the profusion of deep blue berries along tracksides and across the forest floor quickly catches the ye of most trampers. These vary greatly from a rather faded old china blue or white to the deepest and most ivid purple. Walkers frequently pick stalks for the vase only to find the berries falling like droplets of water at ne lightest touch – a likely origin of the name, from rutu, turu or turuturu ('to drip'). When squeezed, these erries produce an inky juice, inspiring the alternative name, **inkberry**. When not yet in flower or fruit, though, Jrutu could easily be mistaken for a grass; however, the fan-shaped arrangement of its leaves provides a clue o the plant's close relationship to New Zealand flax, which belongs to the same Order: Liliales. The berries f its Australian counterpart, *Dianella caerulea*, are recorded as having been eaten by aboriginal Australians, ut the berries of the New Zealand plant are not and were even implicated in the death of an infant in the ate 1800s. Tūrutu berries are nevertheless eaten by birds (including chickens). No part has been recorded s having been used in Māori medicine. Children used to fold the leaves into a tube and blow through it to roduce an ear-splitting whistle. Indeed, in some districts, the plant has even been known as 'whistles'. The enus name, *Dianella*, comes from 'Diana', the name of the Roman goddess of the moon, originally a woodland oddess. Two similar new species have recently been discovered in northern New Zealand (*D. haematica* and *). latissima*).

**Nature Notes:** Berries may be eaten by silvereyes. The plant supports tiny grubs of a native 'turutu leafminer veevil' (*Microcryptorhynchus* species), which mine fine tunnels within the leaves.

**Growing It:** Planted in gardens for its brief show of bright blue berries. Best grown in partial shade in a deep, noist but well-drained soil, either along the borders of a path or as groundcover beneath trees. Propagated by eed or division.

# Mīkoikoi
# New Zealand Iris

*Libertia ixioides* and *L. grandiflora* [Family: Iridaceae]

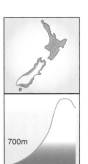

| | |
|---|---|
| **Leaves:** | *Turning yellow to orange in full sun*, smooth, stiff, 30–60 cm long. Growing in fans, forming a tuft |
| **Flowers:** | White, three-petalled (late spring) |
| **Fruit:** | *Yellow, pear-shaped capsules* (autumn and winter) |
| **Other:** | Seen along tracksides and the sides of streams |

The leaves often look striking, especially where growing in full sun, for they then turn a yellow green or golden orange. Koi ('pointed') describes the straight, erect leaves, which are often marked with a distinct orange, spear-like stripe along them, pointed at both ends. (As to whether the 'ī' in 'mī' is a long vowel, there seems to be no agreement.) Other tribal names for the plant include **mānga-a-Huripapa** and **tūkāuki**. The fragile, white, three-petalled flowers may bear little resemblance to those of the garden iris, yet these plants belong to the same family. In fact, the native iris is rarely noticed for its flowers at all – more for its attractive display of long-lasting yellow seed capsules. In nineteenth century New Zealand, these tough leaves were recommended for paper-making. The president of the Edinburgh Botanical Society, in a talk in the Scottish capital in 1880, even promoted growing this plant in Scotland. There are two similar species (and also two much smaller species, *L. pulchella* and *L. peregrinans*). The two larger species can usually be distinguished when the plants are in fruit; the flower stalk of *Libertia grandiflora* is generally longer than its leaves; while the stalk of *L. ixioides* is usually shorter than its leaves.

**Nature Notes:** Flowers produce large quantities of nectar, attracting native bees, which are believed to act as pollinators. These bees are black and do not live in hives but in burrows in the ground. *Libertia ixioides*, at least, is known to support a 'mīkoikoi leafminer weevil' (*Microcryptorhynchus* species) whose tiny grubs chew fine tunnels within the leaves.

**Growing It:** Grown for its attractive flowers and fruit; quite widely used in borders and rock gardens and as groundcover. Easy to propagate by division of larger clumps or from seed. Fairly hardy. Prefers well-drained soil; will grow in open sun or under the light shade of trees and shrubs.

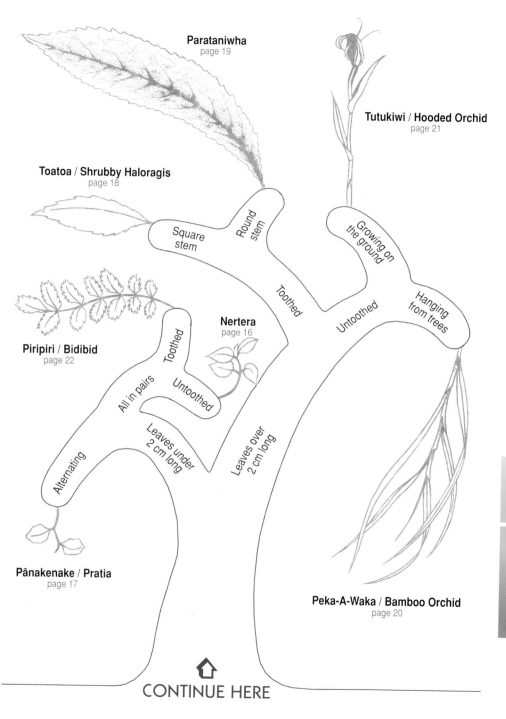

Parataniwha
page 19

Tutukiwi / Hooded Orchid
page 21

Toatoa / Shrubby Haloragis
page 18

Square stem

Round stem

Growing on the ground

Toothed

Untoothed

Hanging from trees

Piripiri / Bidibid
page 22

Nertera
page 16

Toothed

All in pairs

Untoothed

Leaves under 2 cm long

Leaves over 2 cm long

Alternating

Pānakenake / Pratia
page 17

Peka-A-Waka / Bamboo Orchid
page 20

GROUNDCOVERS   PERCHING

⌂
CONTINUE HERE

YOU CAN MEASURE YOUR LEAF HERE    ├── 2 cm ──┤

15

# Nertera

*Nertera depressa* and *N. dichondrifolia* [Family: Rubiaceae]

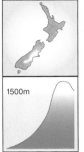

1500m

| | |
|---|---|
| **Leaves:** | Opposite, tiny, egg-shaped or heart-shaped, 5–12 mm long |
| **Fruit:** | *Red, small and round (summer and autumn)* |
| **Other:** | *Creeping to form patches up to 40 cm across in forest, scrub, grass or boggy ground). N. dichondrifolia has hairy leaves* |

At its best, Nertera can form a bright carpet of tiny red berries covering banks and old stumps like scattered beads of a broken necklace, a feature that gave rise to its alternative name, **bead plant**. Although such a conspicuous plant is certainly likely to have been given a Māori name, none has been recorded. There is no record either of its berries having been eaten by Māori, but several people, including myself, have eaten them. They taste rather watery but are otherwise more palatable than many fruit known to have been eaten by Māori. Whether anyone has eaten the berries in sufficient quantity to prove anything about their edibility is doubtful. Like karamū (page 52), Nertera belongs to the coffee family. There are five similar forest species, all of which grow on the moist, forest floor. These can be conveniently divided between those that have hairy leaves and those that do not. A common example of a hairy-leaved kind is *Nertera dichondrifolia* (featured); while *N. depressa* (top right) is a common example of the hairless kind. The leaf blades of the former are about as long as wide; the leaves of the latter are longer than wide.

**Nature Notes:** Grazed by deer. Many forest birds are wary of feeding on the ground, yet the fruit are nevertheless eaten by kererū (New Zealand pigeon) and – on remote off-shore islands (such as Auckland Island) – by New Zealand pipits. Insects so far found on the plant include a native 'seed bug' (*Woodwardiana evagorata*) and the introduced 'greedy scale' and the caterpillars of the 'southern litter looper' (*Homodotis falcata*) which feed on the live leaves.

**Growing It:** The species most commonly grown in gardens is the slightly larger-fruited *Nertera depressa*. Covered in colourful red fruit, this makes an attractive groundcover in rock gardens or along moist banks. Overseas, it is grown in conservatories. Needs a moist soil, but is not particular about sun or shade. Hardy. Easy to grow by division, but can also be grown from seed.

# Pānakenake
# Pratia

*Lobelia angulata* [Family: Campanulaceae]

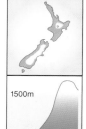

1500m

**Leaves:** Alternating, small, rounded and bluntly toothed

**Flowers:** *White, starry 'half-flowers', larger than the leaves* (late spring to early autumn)

**Fruit:** Purplish red, often at least as big as the leaves (late spring to early winter)

**Other:** *Forming matted patches up to 1 m across*

This plant's Māori name links its appearance with that of a fishing net (nake) – a likeness that can indeed sometimes be quite striking. Pratia carpets the ground along many damp, shaded forest tracksides and the banks of streams, most often catching the tramper's attention with its unusual lop-sided white flowers and purplish red berries. The fact that the blossoms and fruit are both often noticeably larger than the leaves makes the plant eye-catching. The irregular shape of these flowers provides a clue to the fact that pratia is a member of the same family as the garden lobelia. Elsdon Best records that Māori of the Tūhoe tribe of the Urewera district gathered the tiny leaves to cook as greens. Plants have three gender possibilities: they can be either male or female or both – something to bear in mind if you are planting pratia for its attractive fruit.

**Nature Notes:** Careful observations to investigate the pollination of the flowers reveal that they are visited by native flies (particularly hover flies), small native bees and several small moths. The juicy purplish red fruit is sometimes eaten by birds, including pūtangitangi (paradise shelduck). Tiny maggots of the 'pratia leafminer fly' (*Scaptomyza* species) mine young leaves, leaving yellowed patches in them and a white deposit on the leaf surface.

**Growing It:** Planted for its pretty white flowers and reddish berries as a groundcover or rock-garden plant. Hardy. Easily grown; prefers a good, slightly moist soil and full sun or light shade only. Spreads quickly once established, but can easily be trimmed back if necessary. Easy to propagate by cuttings or by division of plants, but can also be raised from seed. Slugs and snails can be a problem. In 1910, it was described as thriving in the Edinburgh Botanic Garden in dry sandy soil in the full sun, forming a close carpet on the soil, making a perfect sheet of white blossom during the Scottish summer.

# Toatoa
# Shrubby Haloragis

*Haloragis erecta* [Family: Haloragaceae]

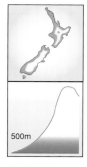

500m

| | |
|---|---|
| **Leaves:** | *Opposite, coarsely toothed, 2.5–5 cm long* |
| **Flowers:** | Inconspicuous |
| **Other:** | *With square, reddish stems.* Can grow to waist height or more, sometimes appearing almost shrub-like. Seen along forest edges and tracksides |

The Māori name is confusing since it is also commonly applied to a kind of celery pine (*Phyllocladus toatoa*), but there is no apparent similarity between the two plants. On account of the plant's long, sharply toothed leaves and the fact that this herb often grows in forest clearings, shrubby haloragis has, more than once, been confused with marijuana and been presented by a farmer to the local police station. That was in the 1970s; however, marijuana is now much better known. Commonly found along the edges of forest, on banks, cliffs and roadsides, shrubby haloragis does indeed look more typical of an exotic species than most native plants and is still often confused for an introduced weed. Juice squeezed from the plants or the liquid from its steeped leaves was used in the nineteenth century for all types of lymphatic tuberculosis. Its seeds were taken to England at least as early as 1778 and, a decade later, toatoa was being grown at the Royal Botanic Gardens at Kew in London and was by 1814 even being offered for sale in the United Kingdom. Since it looks rather weedy and produces no significant flowers, it did not, however, prove popular.

**Nature Notes:** Conspicuous insects found on the plant include caterpillars of a native looper moth (*Epicyme rubropunctaria*) and those of an introduced leaf-tyer moth (the 'lightbrown apple moth'), which webs the leaves together to feed on. Specialist insects supported by the plant include a 'Haloragis leafminer moth' (*Zapyrastra* species), a 'Haloragis gall mite' (*Aceria victoriae*) and a 'Haloragis stem weevil' (*Rhadinosomus acuminatus*).

**Growing It:** Not used in cultivation; although a sprawling subspecies (subsp. *cartilaginea,* native to cliffs at North Cape), which bears shorter, small, round leaves, does make an attractive cascading pot plant.

# Parataniwha

*Elatostema rugosum* [Family: Urticaceae]

1000m

**Leaves:** 8–25 cm long, alternating, coarsely toothed. *Reddish when young; purple-green when older*, with dark veins

**Flowers:** Inconspicuous

**Other:** Grows along streamsides and in damp shaded forest, where the leaves often lie ankle-deep (though they can sometimes be knee-high or more)

With its very striking reddish leaves, this plant attractively clothes the wet forest banks of many North Island backsides and streamsides. Some features, such as its juicy stems, give it a begonia-like look. Its growth habit and sharply serrated leaves are distinctive; these sharp teeth are reminiscent of sharks (taniwha), seeming to hang like the fronds of a fern (para). Europeans also likened the plant to a fern, giving it the popular name begonia fern, yet the plant has no botanical affinity to either fern or begonia, belonging rather to the nettle family. Fortunately it lacks the stinging hairs of better-known members of the family. The reddish colouring of young leaves is due to *anthocyanins,* which are thought to shield the plant from the damaging effects of strong sunlight. Under laboratory conditions, at least, these compounds act as powerful antioxidants, protecting young leaves from environmental stress. Tests also indicate the leaves possess anti-bacterial properties. Māori used the plant for flavouring kūmara, wrapping tubers in leaves prior to cooking in a hāngī; in Australia, the leaves of its local equivalent, 'rainforest spinach' (*Elatostema reticulatum*), are actually eaten.

**Nature Notes:** Conspicuous insects found on the plant include wriggling, looper caterpillars of the 'dusky nettle angle' moth (*Udea marmarina*).

**Growing It:** Though rarely planted in gardens, it is eye-catching in cultivation and easy to grow. Its usefulness comes from its tolerance of moist or shady situations, such as beneath trees or in a fern garden, the main ornamental feature being its range of leaf colour – from wine red to yellow-green, patterned with darker veining. It self-seeds readily but is also easily propagated by division. It is hardier than its natural distribution would suggest, being undamaged by frost as far south as Christchurch, so long as it is given some protection beneath overhanging trees.

# Peka-A-Waka
# Bamboo Orchid
*Earina mucronata* [Family: Orchidaceae]

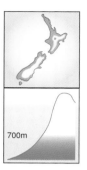

700m

| | |
|---|---|
| **Leaves:** | Straight, grass-like, with black spots on the long sheaths, alternating |
| **Flowers:** | Creamy yellow, *sweet scented*, about 7 mm across, drooping in long sprays of about 40 (in spring) |
| **Other:** | *Growing on tree trunks or hanging from the forks of trees, with drooping, bamboo-like stems* |

'Peka' means 'branch', for this is where the orchid grows. To grow up here in forest trees it employs special tactics to retain moisture: the covering of the roots is pierced with many tiny holes that fill almost instantly in the briefest downpour. This water is passed on for storage in special holding cells for later use — a mechanism that gives the plant the capacity to grow among nests of perching plants in the tops of trees, or hanging from trunks, or directly on rocks apparently devoid of soil.

**Nature Notes:** Hihi (stitchbirds) have been known to visit the flowers for the copious supply of nectar, but the fragrant spring flowers are primarily attracting insects. Indeed, this orchid is believed to be almost completely dependent on flies, beetles and wasps or bees to provide for its pollination. To ensure each insect carries away a good mass of pollen to pollinate the next flower it visits, it receives a dab of quick-drying glue on its forehead. On the other hand, the seeds depend on wind for transport. Leaves are collected as nesting material by forest birds. In the case of the kōkako, however, at least some of the leaves collected are actually being eaten. A lichen is common on the leaves.

**Growing It:** Available from some specialist native plant nurseries. Needs to be tied to a tree trunk or onto a slab of fern fibre, in a position exposed to a fair amount of light. Sphagnum moss tucked in around the roots stimulates growth. It can also be grown in a suitable crevice as part of a rock garden. Also recommended as a pot plant. Tolerant of cold, but requires some filtered sunlight to flower well. More spectacular, both as regards the size and fragrance of its flowers, is the less-common **Easter orchid** (**raupeka**, *Earina autumnalis*) – right.

**PERCHING**

# Tutukiwi
# Hooded Orchid

*Pterostylis banksii* [Family: Orchidaceae]

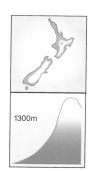

1300m

**Leaves:** Alternating, grass-like

**Flowers:** *Green, with white stripes, hooded* (spring and early summer)

**Other:** Stems up to 45 cm high. Common in native forest, especially along tracksides

The Māori name likens the profile of the flower to the body and long beak of a kiwi, pushing its way through a noose (tutu) formed by the flower's pinkish, antennae-like lowermost petals (see photo). It is a fascinating exercise to get down on your hands and knees to carefully set the orchid's pollination trigger off with a light touch of your finger. See below (Nature Notes) for details. The flower can reset itself within a quarter of an hour. This orchid belongs to a group commonly known as greenhoods – on account of the colour and shape of their flowers. At least 30 species are currently recognised in New Zealand, of which this species is the largest and most conspicuous.

**Nature Notes:** The flowers possess an ingenious trigger mechanism that they use to ensure cross-pollination. An insect landing on the lip of the flower trips the plant's catapult, tossing the potential pollinator inside. As the insect makes its way out again, it has to climb over the flower's sticky stigma, leaving behind any pollen that it might have collected from its last visit to a hooded orchid. Next, the insect receives a smear of adhesive on its body as it squeezes past the flower's glue-secreting gland before brushing against the flower's pollen duster (anther). This cunning set-up ensures that the flower is pollinated, but not with the pollen from its own flower, and that some of its own pollen is carried to other flowers. Insects that have so far been observed visiting these flowers are mostly small, winged insects, including small gnats and mosquitoes, but it is possible that the flowers are being pollinated by spiders too, for several have also been recorded here.

**Growing It:** Not commonly grown but can be cultivated as a rock garden plant or preferably grouped in pots. Greenhoods can (with difficulty) be grown from seed, but are easiest to propagate from offset tubers taken from near the parent plant. Apart from the problem of slugs and snails, they are easy to grow, preferring a shady or semi-shady situation and an open, humus-rich soil.

# Piripiri
# Bidibid

*Acaena anserinifolia* [Family: Rosaceae]

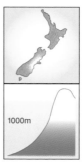

1000m

| | |
|---|---|
| **Leaves:** | Opposite, 4.5–8 cm long, with 9–13 toothed, opposite leaflets, each up to 1 cm long |
| **Flowers:** | Usually white, *like a spiky ball* (late spring) |
| **Fruit:** | *A ball of green burrs, turning reddish-brown* (summer) |
| **Other:** | The burrs attach themselves very readily to clothing |

The Māori name for this plant was brought here from east Polynesia, where it applies to similar burr plants – derived from 'piri' meaning 'to stick to'. 'Bidibid' is a European corruption of this, a name that subsequently crossed the Tasman Sea to give the local Australian equivalent of this plant (sheep's burr) the nickname bidgee-widgee. Alternative Māori names: **pirikahu** ('to stick to clothing'), **huruhuru-o-Hine-nui-te-pō** ('the bristles of Hine-nui-te-pō, daughter of Tāne, goddess of the night') and **piriwhetau** ('the small piri') all refer to these same bristly seed balls. As every farmer knows, this plant has no problem dispersing these barbed seeds, for they get tangled in the wool of sheep, seriously reducing the value of the fleece. Likewise, the spines can become so deeply embedded in the clothing of trampers and picnickers, so as to be almost impossible to remove. It seems surprising then to learn that in 1780 piripiri seeds were actually taken to England *on purpose* and that the plant ended up being recommended both there and in the USA as a good indoor and groundcover plant; and that in Germany hanging baskets of piripiri are often displayed for the ornamental appeal of the reddish flower heads. Medicinally, the boiled or steeped leaves were placed on open wounds and the liquid drunk as a remedy for rheumatism, stomach troubles, kidney and bladder complaints and venereal disease. The dried leaves have also been used as a simple substitute for China tea and as a tonic. The plant has also been used for dyeing wool yellowish-green. Though not technically a forest species, piripiri is nevertheless common along forest tracksides.

**Nature Notes:** Before ground mammals arrived in New Zealand, seeds were presumably transported on the feathers of ground birds such as kiwi and weka. The 'piripiri mealybug' (*Paracoccus acaenae*) feeds on the roots.

**Growing It:** In spite of its popularity overseas, it is generally regarded within New Zealand as being too weedy for cultivation. Some of the alpine species are, however, grown and are usually propagated by division or from cuttings though they can also be raised from seed.

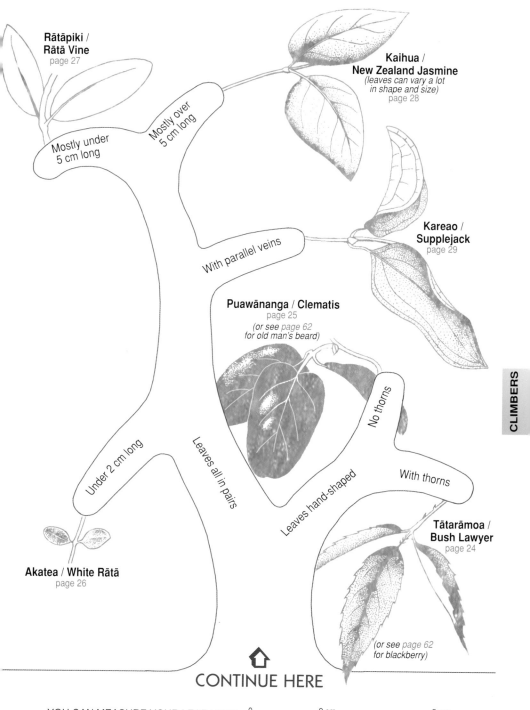

**Rātāpiki /
Rātā Vine**
page 27

**Kaihua /
New Zealand Jasmine**
*(leaves can vary a lot
in shape and size)*
page 28

Mostly under
5 cm long

Mostly over
5 cm long

**Kareao /
Supplejack**
page 29

With parallel veins

**Puawānanga / Clematis**
page 25
*(or see page 62
for old man's beard)*

No thorns

With thorns

Under 2 cm long

Leaves all in pairs

Leaves hand-shaped

**Akatea / White Rātā**
page 26

**Tātarāmoa /
Bush Lawyer**
page 24

*(or see page 62
for blackberry)*

⌂
CONTINUE HERE

YOU CAN MEASURE YOUR LEAF HERE  0    2 cm    5 cm

**CLIMBERS**

# Tātarāmoa
# Bush Lawyer
*Rubus cissoides* [Family: Rosaceae]

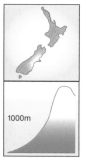

1000m

| | |
|---|---|
| **Leaves:** | *Hand-shaped with 3–5 toothed 'fingers', each 5–13 cm long* |
| **Flowers:** | White, heavily scented (late spring) |
| **Fruit:** | Yellowish-red, shaped like a small blackberry (summer and early autumn) |
| **Other:** | *Branchlets and backs of leaf stalks covered in hooked thorns.* Commonest lawyer species |

Named tātara-a-moa after the prickly 'nicker vine' of east Polynesia, 'tara' in this and alternative tribal names meaning 'thorn'; with 'heke' in **taraheke** and **tātaraheke** meaning 'to climb'. Like the lawyer vine of Australia (also known as 'wait-a-while'), the European and Māori names of the New Zealand plant refer to the tenacious, backward-pointing hooks that snag clothing or skin, bringing passing trampers to an abrupt halt. These same grappling hooks provide this vine with the means to climb from the forest floor to a patch of canopy sunlight. The thorns and fruit are a clue that bush lawyers are close relatives of the common blackberry (page 62). The fruit was eaten by Māori, especially by children; European settlers used them in preserves and jam. In an emergency, the vine can also be cut to extract the thirst-quenching sap. The bark, root bark and leaves were used in Māori medicine. In the 1870s, older thornless lengths of vine were recommended for basket-making and the flowers tipped as a likely commercial source of perfumes.

**Nature Notes:** Flowers visited by stitchbirds, moths, beetles, bristle flies, weevils and thrips. Flowerbuds are eaten by kererū and possums; fruit by geckos, skinks, kōkako and kiwi. Conspicuous insects here include at least five species of stick insects, four native longhorn beetles (including one, *Astetholea pauper*, whose grub apparently specialises in feeding under the bark of bush lawyers) and four moth caterpillars (including those of the 'bush lawyer snoutlet fruit moth', *Heterocrossa rubophaga*, in flowers, fruit and young shoots; the 'lawyer pug' (*Elvia glaucata*) and 'blackheaded leafroller' on leaves). Other specialists include two 'bush lawyer mites', three 'bush lawyer gall midges' and a 'bush lawyer weevil'. Vines are browsed by goats, deer and (especially in winter) possums.

**Growing It:** Grown for its generous clusters of white flowers. For this, the male vine is best, though to have fruit both sexes must of course be grown. (To retain the sex of the vine, grow it from cuttings.) Very hardy, growing in almost any soil and situation. Can be used either as a climber or grown like a climbing rose to cover walls or banks.

# Puawānanga
# Clematis

*Clematis paniculata* [Family: Ranunculaceae]

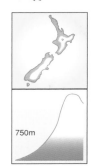

750m

**Leaves:** *Hand-shaped with three 'fingers',* dark, shiny. Lobed when young

**Flowers:** *White, very showy* (late winter and spring)

**Seeds:** Seedheads fluffy (late spring and early summer)

**Other:** Not to be confused with **old man's beard**, which is deciduous and flowers later: December–April (see page 62 )

CLIMBERS

The significance of this flower to Māori is recorded in its name: 'pua' meaning 'flower'; 'wānanga', 'the occult arts'. Elegant headdresses made from flowering wreaths were worn by women. To some tribes, whauwhaupaku (five finger) and puawānanga were the offspring of Puanga (Rigel, the bright star of Orion) and Rehua (Antares, the bright star of Scorpion). The rising of these as morning stars heralded the warmth and plenty of summer. The period between these two events (June to November) coincides with the flowering of five finger and then puawānanga. To climb its forest support, Clematis uses touch-sensitive leaf stalks. When a leaf makes contact with a branch or other object, it coils itself firmly around the support, providing an anchor for the next leg of the vine's ascent. Puawānanga was introduced to Britain in about 1840 and has remained something of a collector's item ever since (grown under glass to protect it from cold winters there). One plant in Massachusetts, USA, is said to have produced 7000 open flowers at a time.

**Nature Notes:** August to October, tūī and honey bees collect nectar. Kōkako consume whole flowers. In spring, kererū eat the leaves. Conspicuous insects include caterpillars of the native 'clematis triangle' moth (a kind of snout moth, *Deana hybreasalis*, top right) and looper caterpillars of the native 'elegant carpet' moth (*Asaphodes chlamydota*, top left). The vine also supports a 'clematis gall midge' and a 'clematis leafminer fly' (*Phytomyza clematadi*). A 'clematis rust fungus' (*Aecidium*) causes twisting and swelling of the stems and leaves. Vines are freely eaten by both goats and deer.

**Growing It:** Regarded as the most beautiful of the native clematis vines. Usually struck from hardwood or semi-hardwood cuttings taken from larger-flowered male vines, but can also be grown from seed (if you don't mind whether your vine is male or female). The flowers do best in full sun, but the roots prefer a certain amount of shade.

# Akatea
# Small White Rātā Vine

*Metrosideros perforata* [Family: Myrtaceae]

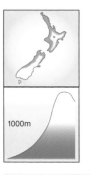

1000m

| | |
|---|---|
| **Leaves:** | *Opposite*, 8–12 mm long, with obvious dots on underside |
| **Flowers:** | *White, fluffy, small* (late summer) |
| **Other:** | Young shoots covered with soft matted hairs. Bark reddish-brown and stringy. (Another very similar-looking small white rātā vine, *M. diffusa*, is more common in some places.) |

'Aka' is a general term for roots and vines; 'tea' means 'white'. Māori used the slender, young vines or rootlets of this plant as lashing. One alternative Māori name **akatoki** refers specifically to its use for lashing adzes (toki). Other names, **torotoro** and **akatorotoro**, refer to the vine's creeping habit. (In Tahitian, 'torotoro' means specifically 'to run or creep as vines'.) The fine clasping roots of young vines provide the means to cling like ivy to trees until they reach the forest canopy, where they can put out more bushy growth. The climbing stem then thickens and swings away from its support to become a woody cable up to 15 cm or more thick. *Metrosideros* (meaning 'iron wood') describes the hard heavy wood; *perforata* refers to glands that dot the undersides of leaves. Recent research confirms that leaves and twigs of this vine possess anti-bacterial properties effective against one of the drug-resistant 'hospital bugs'. More striking, but far less common, is the large-flowered white rātā vine (also known as aka – *Metrosideros albiflora*), from whose inner bark a lotion was made and used by Māori as an antiseptic and to stop bleeding and lessen pain. Sap, obtained by cutting its bark, was used for uterine haemorrhage.

**Nature Notes:** On summer days (January to February), tūī, bellbirds, stitchbirds, native gecko, 'red admiral butterfly' and introduced honey bees visit the flowers; by moonlight, the pale glow of white attracts many species of moth (including the 'brown forest flash', *Pseudocoremia productata*) and beetles (such as the 'speckled longhorn', *Xuthodes punctipennis*) and probably short-tailed bat. Other conspicuous insects found here include at least seven species of native stick insects and looper caterpillars of three species of native moths. This vine also supports a specialist 'akatea scale' insect and a 'rātā rootlet weevil'. In spite of the small leaves, the plant is freely eaten by goats and deer. Kererū (New Zealand pigeons) have been observed eating the leaves of the related *M. diffusa*.

**Growing It:** Grows like ivy from a rooted piece, though the flowers are too small to recommend it in most gardens. Hardy. The much larger-flowered of the white rātā vines, *Metrosideros albiflora*, is another interesting choice, though it too is rarely grown.

# Rātāpiki
# Rātā Vine

*Metrosideros fulgens* [Family: Myrtaceae]

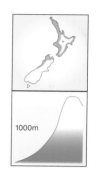

1000m

CLIMBERS

**Leaves:** Opposite, 3–6 cm long

**Flowers:** *Orange-red (mainly autumn and winter)*

**Other:** There are several kinds of red-flowering rātā. This one spends its whole life as a vine; whereas **northern rātā** may start life as a vine but becomes a tree; while **southern rātā** is always a tree

When these flowers open, it is the time to harvest kūmara. Rātā is a tropical east Polynesian name for *Metrosideros* trees, while the specific name rātāpiki distinguishes this rātā as a climber (from 'piki', to climb). Alternative names include **akatawhiwhi** ('aka' for 'roots or vines' and 'tāwhiwhi' meaning 'entwined or entangled'); **akakura** from the red (kura) colouring of the flowers and **kahika** from the likeness of these flowers to those of the tropical Polynesian Malay apple (kahika). Māori used these vines extensively for tying up fences, platforms and the heavy framework of houses. European settlers later used them for making rustic-style garden seats. The vine starts out on the forest floor as a seedling but, on reaching a suitable tree, sends out short roots to latch onto the bark and climb to a sunlit spot, where it sprouts a mass of foliage. The stem will then thicken to supply sufficient water and nutrients, eventually becoming so heavy that it will often swing free of its initial support. Early bushmen would cut a slit in the bark, leaving it hanging to let a thirst-quenching sap drain into a container. In winter, kākā can sometimes be seen tearing the bark to feed in a similar way. This juice is clear or sometimes slightly pink, tasting like dry cider, and was used on wounds too, and for coughs and eye troubles. The bark has been shown to contain *ellagic* acid, an astringent used for dysentery and diarrhoea, while the inner bark was used for healing sores and to stop bleeding. As with pōhutukawa and the two tree rātā, a sweet, pale nectar can be sucked from the flowers.

**Nature Notes:** By day the flowers attract tūī, bellbirds, stitchbirds, kākā, silvereyes and honey bees for nectar, while at night, short-tailed bats visit. A sooty mould on the vine feeds on honeydew excreted by the 'mānuka giant scale' insect (*Coelostomidia wairoensis*). The vine also supports a 'rātā leafminer weevil' (*Neomycta rubida*) and a 'rātā gall mite'. Freely eaten by possums (in spring), goats and deer.

**Growing It:** Cuttings taken from mature bushy growth allow rātā vine to be grown as a shrub; taken from climbing wood it will grow as a climber. Tolerant of cold conditions, though flowerbuds are susceptible to frost damage. Flowers do best in full sun but the roots prefer shade. Easy to grow in fairly rich, well-drained soil.

**27**

# Kaihua
# New Zealand Jasmine

*Parsonsia heterophylla* [Family: Apocynaceae]

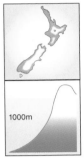

1000m

| | |
|---|---|
| **Leaves:** | Opposite, 5–7 cm long on adult plants. *Leaves on young plants vary a lot in shape and size* |
| **Flowers:** | 6 mm long, white, *sweet scented*, tubular (spring and summer) |
| **Fruit:** | Narrow pod, 7–15 cm long (summer and early autumn) |
| **Other:** | A twining stem climber, often twining about itself. Stems can be as thick as a person's neck |

For details of Māori names, see below. This is another vine used by Māori for tying up fences, platforms and the framework of houses. Although not known to have been used medicinally, alkaloids found in it are believed to have pharmaceutical potential. Vines are easily overlooked since they are frequently draped high over the tops of forest trees; usually, it is the sweet perfume of the flowers that is first noticed, particularly at dusk when a heady scent signals their whereabouts to moths. The vine has a remarkable range of leaf shapes – long or short, broad or narrow, plain or deeply lobed – often all on the same plant; hence the species name, *heterophylla* (different-leaved). This native jasmine should not be confused with the common garden one from China that often grows wild on forest edges, a serious weed in places where it chokes the light from trees. The leaves of the garden species differ in being grouped seven (sometimes five) together, rather than singly (like the native one), with flowerbuds usually pink, rather than white.

**Nature Notes:** Flowers visited at night by many species of moth; by day by flies and a kind of leaf beetle. Seeds eaten by kōkako and kiore (Pacific rats), hence the Māori names, **akakiore**, **akakaikiore** and kaihua ('bearing an edible product'). Leaves are devoured by New Zealand pigeons (kererū, or kūkū of Tainui), hence **kaikūkū**. Conspicuous insects found on the plant include the Australian 'swan plant seed bug' (*Arocatus rusticus*) and eight kinds of 'longhorn beetles' (including two so far known only from this plant). Hold leaves up to the light to see tunnels made inside them by tiny caterpillars of two kinds of 'kaihua leafminer moths'. The vine also supports a 'kaihua scale insect', a 'kaihua gall mite' and a 'kaihua bark weevil'.

**Growing It:** Grown for its thick clusters of sweetly scented white flowers, it is best trained along trellises or fences, or through a tall shrub or tree. Can be grown from seed, but is usually propagated from cuttings taken from mature vines, thus bypassing the plant's juvenile stage and encouraging earlier flowering. Prefers good soil and shaded roots, so long as the flowers are able to develop in full sun. Tolerant of cold and sea winds.

# Kareao
# Supplejack

*Ripogonum scandens* [Family: Ripogonaceae]

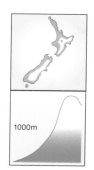

1000m

**Leaves:** *Opposite*, toothless, 7–12 cm long, *with obvious lengthwise parallel veins*

**Fruit:** Bright red, round, 8 mm across (throughout most of the year, but mainly in autumn)

**Other:** Stem twining, usually finger thick, smooth and almost black. The tip looks like a spear of asparagus (not to be confused with the poisonous tutu, page 54)

This vine coils its stems around forest branches or support. If unsuccessful, the vine drops to the ground and tries again, often leaving a tangled mess on the forest floor that can be hard to penetrate. Māori names, kareao or **karewao** ('forest whip'), apparently refer to the way these dense tangles frustrate the progress of 'bush-bashers'. (The equivalent Australian vine in this family, barbwire vine, is worse still, for it has thorns.) Māori split the stems to lash sides and roofs of houses, to secure fences and platforms, as frameworks for masks of birdman kites, woven into crayfish pots, bird cages, snares to catch kiore (Pacific rats), seed-crushing bags, or shields to ward off spears in battle. European settlers used them to make wickerwork, rope ladders and ship's fenders – even tied them to the rims of bicycle wheels as a substitute for pneumatic tyres. The original 'supplejack' is a similarly tough, pliant vine found in the United States, also used for wickerwork. The tender, asparagus-like, growing tips of the local supplejack taste like fresh green beans and can be a useful source of liquid in a survival emergency; these were eaten medicinally as a cure for scabies. (*Take care, however, not to confuse with the poisonous shoots of tutu.*) The thin flesh of the berries was eaten too by Māori, but tastes dry and disappointing. Juice from the boiled roots was used for rheumatism, bowel complaints, fever and skin diseases, later as a substitute for the related South American sarsaparilla as a tonic.

**Nature Notes:** November to January, stitchbirds and bees visit the inconspicuous flowers for nectar. Ripe fruit eaten by tūī, kererū, kōkako, blackbirds, thrushes, deer, pigs and possums (all of which spread the seed). In autumn and winter, kiore and ship rats destroy the seeds. Pigs dig up roots too. Leaves freely eaten by kōkako, bats and possums (especially in winter). Conspicuous insects here include the 'lemon tree borer' (a longhorn beetle) and caterpillars of the native 'sharp-tipped bell moth' (*Epalxiphora axenana*), which webs leaves together.

**Growing It:** Not generally used in cultivation. Very hardy but slow and hard to get established. Can be grown from seed.

# Kiekie

*Freycinetia banksii* [Family: Pandanaceae]

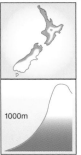

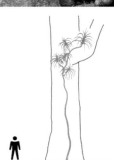

1000m

| | |
|---|---|
| **Leaves:** | 0.5–1 m long, with fine teeth; crowded at end of branches |
| **Flowers:** | 3 cream-coloured fingers amid fleshy white bracts (spring) |
| **Fruit:** | On 3 (sometimes 4) yellow-green, sweetcorn-like 'cobs' (autumn) |
| **Other:** | *Vine as thick as a person's wrist.* Scrambles over rocks and fallen trees, but can reach high into the tops of trees |

'Kiekie' is a term found across most of tropical Polynesia for related *Freycinetia* fibre plants, where it means 'sail' or 'skirt'. In New Zealand, kiekie leaves were used to make rope and to weave coarse clothes, kites, belts, baskets, wall panels, floor and sleeping mats, but also occasionally for sails. The spreading, white flower bracts (**tāwhara**) that surround the flower in spring are juicy with a sweet, fruity taste and are undoubtedly New Zealand's best-tasting wild vegetable food. (Tāwhara means 'spread out' or 'sweet, pleasant to the taste'.) The ripe fruit (**ureure**), that matures in autumn, looks like a green sweetcorn cob, ('ureure' likens the shape to a penis). When ripe to the point of disintegrating, the inner end of the segments of this fruit tastes better than most native plant foods. Both were important to Māori, but are hard to find nowadays – except in areas where pests are being controlled. Common in wet forest and coastal scrub, kiekie clings to its support by wrapping aerial roots around the trunk of its host or inserting these into cracks in the bark. These tough rootlets were valued by Māori as a binding material, used for lashing flutes and adze handles, for example.

**Nature Notes:** Analysis of the fur, stomach and guano of short-tailed bats shows that they visit the flowers and feed on the fruit. Soft flower bracts are also eaten by tūī, kiore, ship rats and possums (which help with pollination). Leaf tufts (even those well above the ground) are known as good places (on Coromandel Peninsula) to find Archey's frog. Ripe fruit is also eaten by silvereyes (tauhou), tūī, kākā, kiore, ship rats, mice and possums. Kōkako and robins collect dead leaf fibre as nesting material. Wilted central leaves result from caterpillars of the 'buff-tipped lily moth' (*Proditrix tetragona*). Other insects include the 'kiekie rootlet weevil' (whose tiny grubs mine live aerial roots); 'kiekie leafminer weevil' (whose grubs mine leaves); and 'kiekie gall midge' (causes small lumps at base of leaves).

**Growing It:** Rarely grown in gardens, but can be planted to scramble over a rock wall, old tree stump or up into tall trees. Hardy, tolerating both direct sun and shade.

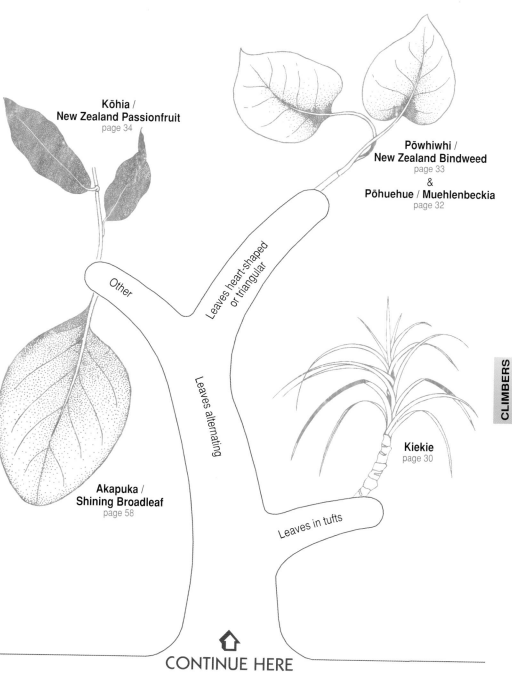

**Kōhia /**
**New Zealand Passionfruit**
page 34

**Pōwhiwhi /**
**New Zealand Bindweed**
page 33
&
**Pōhuehue / Muehlenbeckia**
page 32

Leaves heart-shaped
or triangular

Other

Leaves alternating

Kiekie
page 30

**Akapuka /**
**Shining Broadleaf**
page 58

Leaves in tufts

CLIMBERS

⬆
CONTINUE HERE

# Pōhuehue
# Large-Leaved Muehlenbeckia

*Muehlenbeckia australis* [Family: Polygonaceae]

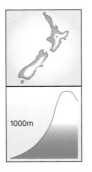

1000m

| | |
|---|---|
| **Leaves:** | *Heart-shaped (young leaves violin-shaped), 2.5–7 cm long, alternating* |
| **Fruit:** | *Tiny black seed, sitting in a white or ice-coloured swollen flower (summer)* |
| **Other:** | A twining stem climber that often clambers over trees and shrubs, sometimes even smothering other vegetation or forming large tangles |

Māori ate the swollen, five-pointed, berry-like blossoms, which taste surprisingly sweet and juicy – particularly popular with children. I have eaten them many times myself. In Australia, the 'fruit' of their native equivalent has been used in pies, puddings and confectionery. In many districts, the smaller-leaved *M. complexa* is more common, but this grows in open country and is not a forest plant. This and *M. axillaris* share the same Māori name and the 'fruits' of both are also edible. The Māori name links all three plants with unrelated vines (pōhue) in the east Polynesian homeland.

**Nature Notes:** The tiny, inconspicuous flowers rely on numbers ('flag effect') to attract small pollinating insects, including at least two species of beetle. Tūī, bellbirds and kererū eat the fruit; kererū and kōkako also eat leaves and buds. Conspicuous insects feeding on the leaves include at least five species of stick insects, green caterpillars of the 'glade copper' (top) and 'common copper' butterfly. Long, kūmara-shaped woody swellings on the stem (right) are the work of the 'pōhuehue gall moth' (*Morova subfasciata*), below. Pimples (pouch-shaped galls) on the upper surface of leaves are likely to be the work of a mite that lays its eggs here. Also conspicuous here are the caterpillars of a 'pōhuehue leafminer moth', five native leaf-tyer moths, three owlet moths (including the 'pōhuehue owlet', *Meterana coeleno*), a looper in the flowers; and the 'pine longhorn' beetle. The vine also supports a 'pōhuehue aphid', a 'pōhuehue psyllid', a 'pōhuehue scale' insect, a 'pōhuehue mirid' and four 'pōhuehue weevils'. Freely eaten by possums.

**Growing It:** None of the muehlenbeckias are commonly grown in gardens. Those that have been recommended for cultivation are *M. astonii*, *M. axillaris* and *M. ephedroides*, all of which can be grown from seed or hardwood cuttings. Their attraction is in their unusual ice-like fruit.

# Pōwhiwhi
# New Zealand Bindweed

*Calystegia tuguriorum* [Family: Convolvulaceae]

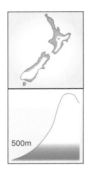

500m

**Leaves:** Alternating, *triangular to heart-shaped*, 1–4 cm long, *on long stalks*

**Flowers:** *Large, funnel-shaped, white* or sometimes pink (late spring and summer)

**Other:** A twining stem climber. Found in scrubland and edges of native forest

Pōwhiwhi means 'wind around', 'tangled' or 'interlaced'; it is a name that is shared with other native vines, including **coastal morning glory** (*Ipomoea cairica*), and **New Zealand passionfruit** (page 34). There are several kinds of bindweed in New Zealand, the others being more common in gardens, waste ground and sand dunes. This native one is usually found sprawling in thick mats over trees and shrubs along the edges of native forest and has smaller leaves than the others. In spite of its local name, it is native also to Chile (including the archipelago de Juan Fernández). The first collection of the plant by botanists was, however, made at Te Oneroa, New Zealand, in October 1769 by Joseph Banks. His party saw it growing near a group of whare (Māori huts), hence the botanical name, *tuguriorum* from 'tugurium', meaning 'hut'. *Calystegia* means 'covered calyx', referring to the green sheaths that cover the bases of the flowers. Some species of vines use thorns or clinging roots to climb their support; others use tendrils or twining leaf stalks; however, bindweeds and honeysuckles both use twining stems. Although honeysuckles climb by twining clockwise, all members of the bindweed family twine anti-clockwise – or so it is said. Being relatively short-lived and weak-stemmed, the vines of this plant are rarely found in hosts taller than nine metres.

**Nature Notes:** Kererū (New Zealand pigeons) eat the leaves and possibly also the flowerbuds and flowers. The native 'bindweed gall mite' makes 'pouch galls' or 'pocket galls' on the leaves of this and other bindweeds. This vine belongs to the family of plants eaten by caterpillars of the 'Convolvulus hawk moth'; however, I am not aware of anyone having found this caterpillar feeding here.

**Growing It:** Rarely used in cultivation, but suited to exposed locations. Resistant to salt and wind, but can also be rather invasive and difficult to eradicate.

# Kōhia
# New Zealand Passionfruit

*Passiflora tetrandra* [Family: Passifloraceae]

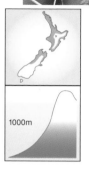

**Leaves:** Alternating, pointed, shiny, up to 6 cm long

**Flowers:** White, *similar to a small garden passionfruit flower* (late spring)

**Fruit:** *Orange, pear-shaped*, about 2.5 cm across (autumn)

**Other:** A tendril climber. Not to be confused with the larger-flowered **banana passionfruit** (page 62), a serious weed in some areas of native forest

Kōhia, **akakōhia** and names like **kaimanu**, **akakaimanu**, **akakūkū** and **akakaikūkū** all refer to the attractiveness of the fruit to birds, from kai (food), manu (bird), aka (vine), kūkū (kererū or pigeon), kō (birdsong) and hia (desire). Māori followed the movements of such birds for food and used this vine for tying up fences, platforms and the framework of houses. The main stem was also valued for carrying fire on long journeys, as this burns particularly slowly. Other Māori names (**pōhue**, **pōhuehue**, **pōpōhue** and **aka**) refer to the plant as a vine; while **pōwhiwhi** means 'wind around', 'tangled' or 'interlaced', referring to the way its tendrils corkscrew around small branches and stems, anchoring it for its ascent to the forest canopy. The orange fruit was eaten by Māori. (Indeed, one name, **akatororaro**, refers to this as a vine (aka) to forage (toro) under (raro). The plant is closely related to the common garden passionfruit, but the fruit of this species is dry and disappointing by comparison. The black seeds were particularly important to Māori – crushed, steamed and pressed to extract an oil that was perfumed with leaves of aromatic plants to make scented body oils. This same oil (which has proven to be rich in *linoleic acid*) was also used medicinally: applied to chronic sores, old wounds and chapped nipples. Māori used a gum-like substance that bleeds from the cut stem, too, as a form of chewing gum.

**Nature Notes:** Nectar is collected by stitchbirds (top left). Kererū (or kūkū, New Zealand pigeons), tūī and kākāriki eat the fruit. Kōkako (top right) eat both fruit and leaves. Possums and ship rats also relish the pulp and seeds. So far, four kinds of weevils and one kind of scale insect have been recorded feeding on the plant.

**Growing It:** Roots readily from cuttings (which allows for selection of male or female plants); also grown from seed. Both sexes must be grown to produce the attractive fruits. Roots prefer cool shade, though flowers prefer to be in full sun. Quick to grow in fairly good soil.

Previously known as *Tetrapathaea tetrandra*.

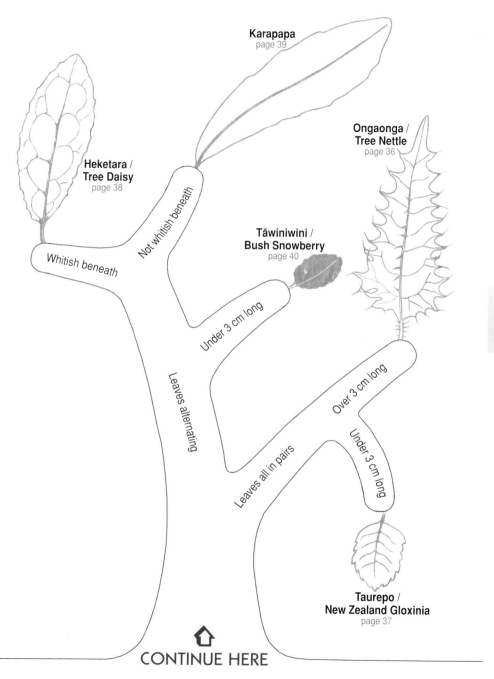

**Karapapa**
page 39

**Ongaonga /
Tree Nettle**
page 36

**Heketara /
Tree Daisy**
page 38

Not whitish beneath

**Tāwiniwini /
Bush Snowberry**
page 40

Whitish beneath

Under 3 cm long

Leaves alternating

Over 3 cm long

Under 3 cm long

Leaves all in pairs

**Taurepo /
New Zealand Gloxinia**
page 37

SHRUBS

⬆
CONTINUE HERE

YOU CAN MEASURE YOUR LEAF HERE ├── 3 cm ──┤

# Ongaonga Tree Nettle

*Urtica ferox* [Family: Urticaceae]

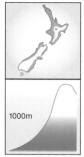

1000m

| | |
|---|---|
| **Leaves:** | 5–12 cm long, opposite, with large teeth, covered with long, very conspicuous, silvery, stinging hairs |
| **Other:** | With lots of branches; *whole plant covered with long stinging hairs*. Found mostly along the edges of forest and in scrub; common near Wellington and Christchurch |

Ongaonga is a term used for stinging nettles throughout most of Polynesia. An alternative name, **taraongaonga**, draws attention to the particular sharpness of the stinging hairs. Considering how DANGEROUS this shrub is, it is surprising how few New Zealanders know it. Not only have several dogs and horses died from coming into contact with it, but it has killed at least one tramper who pushed through a thicket of the plant. The stinging hairs can be 6 mm or more in length, each constructed like a hypodermic syringe. The slightest touch knocks the delicate tip off the needle, leaving a slanting point which drives into the skin. The elastic barrel at the base of the needle immediately shrinks, pumping its venom into the victim. The extract from just five of these fat stinging hairs is sufficient to kill a guinea pig. In severe cases of poisoning, artificial respiration and an intramuscular injection of *atropine* may be necessary. In mild cases, the irritation and pain can be eased with calamine or an antihistamine preparation. Although related to the common garden nettle (with the same toxins), ongaonga also manufactures another poison that has so far defied identification. The much smaller **dwarf bush nettle** (*Urtica incisa*) is also sometimes seen along tracksides, but this is not known to be dangerous.

**Nature Notes:** A whitish pollen is ejected explosively from the inconspicuous flowers. Bees collect a pale, cloudy nectar to make a light, delicately flavoured honey similar to that of thistle. Several caterpillars feed on the plant, including those of the 'red admiral butterfly' (top, right) and of moths (top, left to right), 'rusty dotted triangle', 'dusky nettle triangle', 'tree nettle flash', and 'L-mark ongaonga flash' (*Pseudocoremia flava*); also of 'ongaonga owlet' and 'ongaonga pug'. The plant also supports a 'nettle leafminer fly' that makes blotches in the leaves. In spite of the stinging hairs, plants are nevertheless eaten by goats and deer, but rarely by possums. Wild pigs frequently dig up nettle plants to eat the roots.

**Growing It:** Being unattractive and potentially dangerous, it is not used in cultivation.

# Taurepo
# New Zealand Gloxinia

*Rhabdothamnus solandri* [Family: Gesneriaceae]

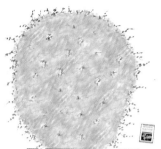

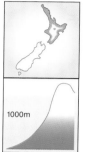

1000m

**SHRUBS**

**Leaves:** *Opposite*, hairy, 1–2 cm long with rounded teeth and dark main veins; sandpapery to touch

**Flowers:** Yellow to orange *with red stripes*, bell-like, 25 mm long and hanging, unscented (mostly spring)

**Other:** Branches opposite, tangled and twiggy. Particularly common by streamsides

'Taurepo' describes the plant as being capable of living in a swamp (repo), while alternative Māori names, kaikaiatua and waiūatua, evoke a sense of something strange or supernatural. Māori are said to have used the leaves and twigs in medicinal vapour baths. Flowering signalled the fourth month of the indigenous calendar (August–September). These flowers are bisexual yet cannot fertilise themselves. This is because the anther (the male part of the flower that carries the pollen) ripens first. At this time, it moves forward to the edge of the flower to dust pollen onto birds that come to feed on the nectar. Later, as that flower matures, this anther bends back again, letting the stigma (the female part of the flower) move forward to take its place. Birds visiting at this time often bring pollen from another flower, dusting this onto the stigma, thus ensuring cross-pollination. The flowers have been shown to contain *anthocyanins* – a type of *glucoside* plant colouring that changes according to the acidity of cell sap (violet when neutral, red if acid and blue when alkaline). Plants growing on offshore islands, such as Little Barrier Island, frequently have far larger leaves – up to 6 cm long, occasionally more. The European name refers to the shape of the flowers being similar to a related garden plant.

**Nature Notes:** The tubular flowers are adapted for bird pollination and are an important source of nectar for stitchbirds, tūī and bellbirds – see above details on the pollination benefits and mechanics of such honeyeater visits. However, in areas with roaming cats, birds are often unwilling to feed this close to the ground. The 'taurepo gall midge' causes folded leaf gall and distorted leaves (see bud, top left). Generally avoided by deer.

**Growing It:** Grown for its pretty bell-shaped flowers. It can be raised from seed, but is usually grown from semi-hardwood cuttings (partly because this is the only way to be sure of the flower colour). Prefers light shade and rich, well-drained soil. Somewhat frost-sensitive. Pruning encourages a more bushy shape and increases the number of flowers.

# Heketara
# Tree Daisy

*Olearia rani* [Family: Asteraceae]

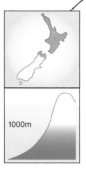

1000m

**Leaves:** *Almost white beneath* with darker veins, stiff, with irregular teeth, *alternating*, 5–15 cm long

**Flowers:** White, *daisy-like*, in clusters (spring)

**Other:** Branchlets covered in soft, pale hairs. (Note that this common species is just one of several kinds of tree daisy.)

The name 'heketara' describes the toothed leaves, while the alternative Māori name, **wharangi piro**, apparently refers to the scent or smell ('piro') and to what is thought to be the origin of the species name, *rani* (a corruption of wharangi). Elsdon Best states that Māori used these leaves for scenting oil, making neck sachets, or perfuming a house when visitors were expected, but personally, I have never been able to detect anything attractive in the scent; it smells to me little different from mown grass. Until the 1960s this plant was often suspected of poisoning stock, but feeding trials on sheep and rats led researchers to conclude that it is in fact quite harmless. The wood was occasionally used during the nineteenth century by cabinetmakers, and described as 'light-coloured, compact and satiny, with a very fine silver grain and small figure'. As the shrub's English common name and its many-petalled flowers suggest, heketara is a member of the daisy family. It is a relative, too, of the better-known and rather similar-looking native tree rangiora (which generally has larger and much softer leaves).

**Nature Notes:** In moonlight, the clusters of white flowers flag the attention of moths and beetles. By day, the flowers are useful to beekeepers, producing in good years large quantities of yellowish pollen in September and October. Other conspicuous insects found on the plant include the native 'giraffe weevil' and the caterpillars of three native 'leafminer moths' that chew tunnels inside the leaves. Holes in young leaves are caused by a native 'leaf beetle' (these jump like a flea). The plant also supports two 'heketara weevils', one whose grubs tunnel under the dead bark (*Hoplocneme* species) and one whose grubs bore into the sound wood (*Didymus bicostatus*); an 'Olearia flower weevil' whose grubs live in the flowers, a 'heketara mealybug' that lives on the roots, and an 'Olearia psyllid'.

**Growing It:** Valued for its prolific show of white flowers. Easiest to propagate from cuttings, but can be grown from fresh seed. Prefers a fairly good soil and tolerates light shade. Reasonably hardy when mature.

# Karapapa

*Alseuosmia macrophylla* [Family: Alseuosmiaceae]

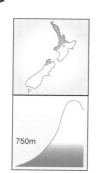

750m

**Leaves:** Alternating, 7–18 cm long, often glossy, *with widely spaced teeth*

**Flowers:** Crimson or cream, fragrant, hanging, *trumpet-shaped*, 3–4 cm long (spring)

**Fruit:** Crimson, 8–11 mm long (summer)

**Other:** With reddish-brown branchlets. (A close relative, *A. pusilla* is often confused with mountain horopito – page 60)

The plant's botanical name, *Alseuosmia*, comes from the Greek for a perfumed grove. The long, trumpet-shaped flowers give off a most delicious fragrance during their short season – a sweet perfume that has led some to call this plant **bush daphne**, but, apart from the similarity of the scent, there is no close relationship. This scent ('kara') is likewise alluded to in the Māori name; with 'papa' meaning 'lying flat or thrown down', as does the alternative name, **toropapa**, which means 'to lie flat' – both appropriate names for a plant that is frequently found growing low to the ground. The ripe berries taste very sweet, yet I have found no record of their having been traditionally eaten by Māori. On one occasion, when testing the possibility of surviving solely on wild plant food by tramping the Coromandel Range for 10 days with no food supplies, this is one of the fruits I ate in large quantities. I was lucky that summer, it seems, for such heavy fruiting occurs only once every four years. An extract of the leaves has been shown to have anti-bacterial properties against so-called 'hospital superbugs' (drug-resistant bacteria).

**Nature Notes:** In September and October, the nectar attracts hihi (stitchbirds), korimako (bellbirds) and honey bees. Indeed, the plant is said to rarely set much viable seed, except where native nectar-feeding birds are common – such as on rodent-free offshore islands. However, birds generally have a poor sense of smell, so the strong scent of the flowers suggests that insects are in fact major pollinators. The fruit is eaten by kākāriki (yellow-crowned parakeets). The shrub supports at least two specialist insects: a 'karapapa psyllid' (*Trioza alseuosmiae*, which causes pitted marks on the leaves – above) and a 'karapapa weevil' (whose grubs live in dead branches). Plants are often heavily browsed by goats, deer and possums.

**Growing It:** Grown in gardens for the perfume and beauty of its flowers. Will not tolerate direct sunlight. Needs a well-drained soil with plenty of peat or leaf-mould. Easy to grow from semi-hardwood cuttings.

# Tāwiniwini
# Bush Snowberry

*Gaultheria antipoda* [Family: Ericaceae]

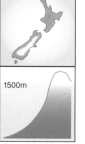

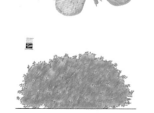

1500m

| | |
|---|---|
| **Leaves:** | *Alternating*, 8–16 mm long, *almost round, toothed*, shiny |
| **Flowers:** | White, bell-shaped (late spring and summer) |
| **Fruit:** | Red or white (summer and early autumn) |
| **Other:** | Sometimes stunted to just a few centimetres high, especially where growing in exposed or rocky places |

The nickname, **fool's beech**, refers to the fact that the leaves are easily mistaken for those of silver beech.

The fruits (technically, the swollen fleshy calyx) of this and the related **mountain snowberry** (*Gaultheria depressa*) were eaten by pre-European Māori. Several early European explorers also expressed gratitude for them when other food supplies gave out. A. J. Barrington, for example, while on a prospecting trip along the West Coast of the South Island in 1863–64, wrote: 'I was so weak that I thought I must give in, but I ate plenty of the little snow-berries [the mountain species] which grow under the snow. They helped us on a good deal . . .' A similar focus is found in the plant's Māori names, some of which suggest that (as in English) the terms were first coined for the mountain species. This is particularly so of tāwiniwini ('relieved of dread'); alternative Māori names include **taupuku** ('edible'), **takapo** ('heaps in the right season'), **tahupāpapa** ('plenty of food on the ground'). Depending on the conditions in which the plants grow, the taste varies a good deal, from dry and tasteless to sweet and juicy. Folk in Otago and Southland even used to collect the fruits to bake snowberry pies – something I have yet to try. The leaves were used medicinally, either boiled as a decoction or raw as a poultice on wounds. An infusion was also used to treat asthma.

**Nature Notes:** Between September and November, honey bees collect a dark-coloured nectar from the flowers. At night, geckos and skinks eat the fruit; by day kererū (New Zealand pigeons) and weka (top right). The plant supports the caterpillars of the 'snowberry yellow' moth (*Orthoclydon chlorias*), a 'snowberry gall mite' (causes galled flowerbuds and a disfiguration of shoots, called 'witches' broom'), a 'snowberry gall midge' (whose grubs live in the flowerbuds) and tiny caterpillars of two 'snowberry leafminer' moths (that tunnel inside the leaves).

**Growing It:** Planted for its showy berries. Prefers a rich, moist soil. Slow to establish but otherwise easy. Propagated from cuttings or from seed; available from specialist nurseries.

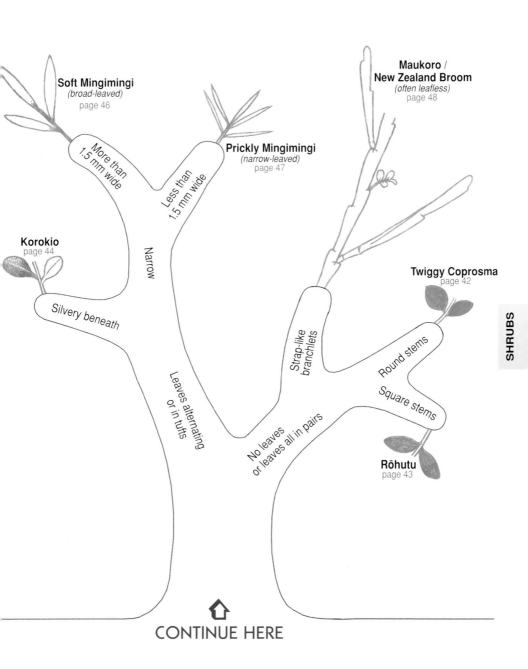

**Soft Mingimingi**
*(broad-leaved)*
page 46

**Maukoro /
New Zealand Broom**
*(often leafless)*
page 48

More than
1.5 mm wide

**Prickly Mingimingi**
*(narrow-leaved)*
page 47

Less than
1.5 mm wide

Narrow

**Korokio**
page 44

**Twiggy Coprosma**
page 42

Silvery beneath

Strap-like
branchlets

Round stems

Square stems

Leaves alternating
or in tufts

No leaves
or leaves all in pairs

**Rōhutu**
page 43

⬆
CONTINUE HERE

YOU CAN MEASURE THE WIDTH OF YOUR LEAF HERE ⊢ 1.5 mm

# Twiggy Coprosma

*Coprosma rhamnoides* [Family: Rubiaceae]

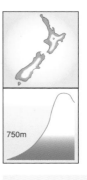

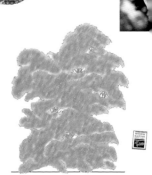

750m

| | |
|---|---|
| **Leaves:** | *Opposite*, 7–12 mm long, with veins visible underneath |
| **Fruit:** | Dark red to black, 4 mm (late summer) |
| **Other:** | *Very twiggy.* Check also for the tell-tale sign of all coprosmas – a tiny, bud-like scale where the leaves meet the stem |

New Zealand has many small-leaved coprosmas (about 30 in all); in native forest and scrubland this is the most common of them. It has a distinctively twiggy appearance – with intertangled branches growing at wide angles to one another. There are two main theories as to why this, and about 60 other native plants, have adopted this strange habit of growth (called divarication). One theory holds that this is the plants' defence against being browsed by moa, since the bulk of inner leaves would have been difficult for those birds to reach and small enough to not be worth the trouble. Equally convincing is an alternative theory which explains that these plants evolved to cope with the climatic upheaval of the Ice Ages, effectively sheltering their leaves from strong winds, frost and drought. In either case, a puzzle remains as to why this habit of growth is almost solely confined to New Zealand. Tests in 1918 discovered that a good, fast, orange wool dye can be made from the bark; however, it was not long before the industrial importance of indigenous plant dyes was eclipsed by the availability of cheaper synthetic varieties.

**Nature Notes:** Wind pollinated. Berries eaten at night by geckos and skinks (especially on offshore islands); by day by tūī, bellbirds (korimako), kererū, stitchbirds, weka and ship rats. The tangled growth habit continues to be effective today in protecting the plant from browsing deer, goats and cattle. Conspicuous insects here include native caterpillars of the 'dark coprosma carpet' moth (*Austrocidaria similata*, top middle), 'coprosma pug' moth (*Pasiphila sandycias*), and one 'pallid coprosma leafroller' (*Leucotenes coprosmae*, top left); a 'coprosma leaf beetle' (chews holes in young leaves in spring and can jump like a flea). The shrub also supports two kinds of 'coprosma gall mite', several specialist 'coprosma gall midges', two 'coprosma scale' insects and a 'coprosma whitefly'.

**Growing It:** Not normally grown in gardens, but will root readily from semi-hardwood cuttings. Also easy to grow from seed. Hardy.

# Rōhutu

*Neomyrtus pedunculata* [Family: Myrtaceae]

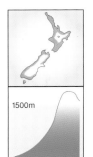

1500m

**Leaves:** Mostly egg-shaped, pale, *covered with glands, opposite*, 6–12 mm long

**Flowers:** White, like a miniature rātā flower, on a long slender flower-stalk (summer)

**Fruit:** Red to yellow, 6 mm, on long thin stalks (autumn)

**Other:** A twiggy shrub with *square-angled*, hairless branchlets; bark very pale

A common plant of both native forest and scrub country, this is easily confused with some of the small-leaved coprosmas – like the species on the facing page – but the square-angled branchlets of rōhutu are distinctive. The Māori names, rōhutu and **rōutu** also apply to the similar and closely related *Lophomyrtus obcordata* and are terms that also refer to a 'comb made of the wood' of these shrubs. Although small, the berries were nevertheless eaten by Māori. Opinions as to their importance differ. Johannes Anderson suggests they were eaten only when better fruit was hard to find. However, the Rev. William Colenso described them not only as 'good to eat', but states that Māori collected them in quantity, explaining how they did so by placing clothes or floor mats beneath the shrubs and shaking the fruit onto them. As the brush-like flowers suggest, rōhutu shares the myrtle family with rātā, pōhutukawa, feijoa and guava. The ripe berries have since been shown to contain *anthocyanins* which laboratory evidence has confirmed can be effective against cancer and diabetes. The dense wood is prettily marked and – apart from being used by Māori for combs – was sometimes used for making handles for axes, mallets and chisels. Cross-cut sections of the trunk were occasionally used for inlaying and marquetry.

**Nature Notes:** The fruit is eaten by forest birds including kererū (New Zealand pigeon) and the seeds dispersed by them. The twiggy growth and small leaves, which are likely to have provided an effective defence for the plant against being eaten by moa, now serve to protect it against being browsed by deer and goats. On dairy farms, the same feature explains why it often survives cattle. The plant supports two kinds of specialist 'rōhutu scale insect' and is currently threatened by the arrival in 2017 of an orange-yellow rust fungus known as myrtle rust.

**Growing It:** Not much used in gardens but can be pruned into a dense shrub. Likes a good soil; can be grown from cuttings or from seed.

**43**

# Small-Leaved Korokio

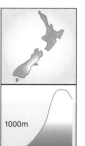

*Corokia cotoneaster* [Family: Argophyllaceae]

1000m

| | |
|---|---|
| **Leaves:** | Spoon-shaped, *2–15 mm long* (not counting the wide stalk), *silvery-white below*, alternating or in tufts |
| **Flowers:** | *Bright yellow, star-like* (mainly spring) |
| **Fruit:** | Bright red to yellow, 6 mm across (late summer) |
| **Other:** | Black bark; tangled, zigzag branches; branchlets silvery |

Can be common on sea cliffs, in lowland mānuka shrubland, in forest, along river flats, stabilised sand dunes and in rocky places, right up to subalpine shrubland. The close relationship between this and the korokio on the opposite page has meant that the two shrubs are often confused. The difference lies largely in the leaves, and this is where the species name (the second half of the botanical name) helps, likening its small leaves to those of the common garden cotoneaster. Now grown in England and in the United States, where the plant is known as the **New Zealand wire-netting bush** or **skeleton plant** – both names referring to the tangle of fine, angled branchlets. In full flower, it is regarded as the highlight of at least one British garden. As with other divaricating shrubs, this tangled growth serves to make the plant uninviting to browsing animals. The plant possesses two features that also give it the ability to survive hot, dry summers: hairs on the underside of the leaves to help retain moisture, and thick woody branches in which the plant can store water. Flowering signalled the fourth month of the Māori calendar (August–September).

**Nature Notes:** In September and November, the hundreds of small starry yellow flowers attract native bees and are a minor but useful source of pale, thin, delicately fragrant nectar for introduced honey bees. The berries are an attractive food for tūī, korimako (bellbirds) and kererū (New Zealand pigeons). Flat-headed caterpillars of the 'korokio looper' (*Horisme suppressaria*) moth feed on the leaves, while caterpillars of two native leaf-tyer moths (including the specialist 'korokio leaf-tyer', *Ericodesma cuneata*) web leaves together.

**Growing It:** Planted for its starry yellow flowers and red, orange or yellowish fruits. Often used as a hedging plant but suitable also as an ornamental shrub. Left unpruned, it grows into a rounded bush about head high. Will withstand the effects of salt wind and dry conditions. Easily rooted from semi-hardwood cuttings but can also be raised from seed.

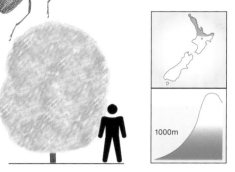

# Korokio Tāranga
# Long-Leaved Korokio

*Corokia buddleioides* [Family: Argophyllaceae]

1000m

| | |
|---|---|
| **Leaves:** | *7–15 cm long*, narrow, *silvery-white below*, alternating |
| **Flowers:** | *Bright yellow, star-like* (late spring) |
| **Fruit:** | Dark red to black, 6 mm long (summer) |
| **Other:** | Black bark; branchlets silvery |

was the Māori name 'korokio' that inspired the botanical name, *Corokia*. Dictionaries record the name for this orokia species only (also the similarly long-leaved koromiko and kiokio fern), suggesting that it was Europeans ho later transferred the name to the small-leaved species, opposite. The epithet, tāranga, is likewise apparently plied only to long-leaved plants. Botanists noted this long leaf-shape too when coining the species name, *uddleioides*, linking this feature with the popular garden buddleia ('butterfly bush'). Apart from this difference in aves, this species also lacks the tangled, zigzag branches. Its habitat is also different, for this long-leaved shrub ll thrive in semi-shade, occurring naturally along forest edges and tracks in the northern North Island, often in uri forest. Drinking the liquid from boiled leaves was said to give instant relief from stomach-ache.

**ature Notes:** The fruit is eaten by birds, most likely tūī, korimako (bellbirds) and kererū (New Zealand pigeons). e flat-headed caterpillars of the 'korokio looper' (*Horisme suppressaria*) moth feed on the leaves. The wood-oring grubs of the 'lemon tree borer' (*Oemona hirta*) tunnel in the branches; in summer these develop into a onspicuous brown native longhorn beetle over 2 cm long (above).

**rowing It:** Planted in shrub borders for its attractive foliage and pretty yellow, star-like flowers. Recommended for ncouraging birds into the garden. Withstands dry conditions. Easily rooted from semi-hardwood cuttings, but can so be raised from seed. When collecting seed, it is important, however, to ensure that the small-leaved korokio n the facing page) is not growing nearby, since the two species hybridise freely. Although it will grow well in the ade of large trees, as a garden plant it is best grown in a sunny situation, though it requires some shelter from nd. This plant is now available in several nurseries in the United Kingdom and in France.

# Mingimingi
# Soft Mingimingi

*Leucopogon fasciculatus* [Family: Ericaceae]

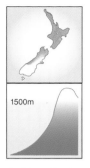

1500m

| Leaves: | Alternating or in tufts, 1–2.5 cm long and *2–4 mm wide*. (Leaves softer than those of tōtara or mānuka, and not as prickly as the narrower-leaved mingimingi, opposite) |
|---|---|
| Flowers: | Tiny, sweet-smelling (spring) |
| Fruit: | Red, *3–4 mm across*, in bundles (spring, summer and autumn) |
| Other: | Black bark |

'Mingimingi' means 'twisted grain'. Known by Ngāi Tahu as **mikimiki**, a name used in the Tuāmotu Archipelago for a shrub with similarly strong, elastic wood. I can find no reliable record of the tiny fruit having been traditionally eaten by Māori, but many bushwalkers, including myself, have eaten them in quantity. Though too small to supply much sustenance, they are juicy, sweet and refreshing. The soft, mānuka-like leaves have been used medicinally by Māori boiled in water and the liquid drunk for headache and influenza. I have used it for headache, with apparent good effect. While plants with female flowers will be heavily laden, others (with bisexual ones) may produce no fruit at all. The long leaf-buds are furled in the shape of a closed umbrella. These features distinguish it from mānuka, which grows in similar places – in shrubland and light forest. On some plants (particularly northern and juvenile ones), and where the shrub is growing in less exposed situations, the leaves can be much larger.

**Nature Notes:** Believed to be pollinated by moths. Silvereyes (tauhou), weka and lizards eat the fruit. Outer branches are a favourite nesting site of silvereyes. Rarely eaten by goats or possums, though plants growing on ridges are frequently marked by possums with horizontal territorial bite marks on the trunks as they rub their scent glands on the shrub. One of the most conspicuous specialist insects found here – at least in the North Island – is the bright green 'Dugdale's cicada' (*Kikihia dugdalei*). Two 'ridge-backed stick insects' feed on the leaves; in summer, I often go out and watch these by torchlight. Caterpillars here include those of the 'common forest looper' and at least six native leaf-tyer moths (including two specialist 'mingimingi leaf-tyers'). 'Pūriri moth' caterpillars feed within the stems. A bright red 'mingimingi mite' feeds on the leaves.

**Growing It:** This mingimingi is not generally cultivated (because the fruit is so small). Hardy and not difficult to grow.

Until recently known as *Cyathodes fasciculata*.

# Mingimingi
# Prickly Mingimingi

*Leptecophylla juniperina* [Family: Ericaceae]

1000m

**Leaves:** Alternating or in tufts, *very prickly to touch*, 6–16 mm long and only 1 mm wide

**Fruit:** Red, pink or white, *5–8 mm across* (throughout most of the year)

**Other:** Black bark. Leaves can be longer on plants growing further south

SHRUBS

...ke the soft mingimingi (opposite), this is a plant of forest and scrubland, particularly on poor soils. Although the ...hite, pink or red fruits are not known to have been a food of Māori, they are often eaten by trampers. The taste is ...veet but often too dry to be satisfying. Some rural children use them as ammunition in peashooters. The small, ...ickly leaves have been used medicinally by Māori, boiled in water for kidney trouble, asthma, menstrual disorders ...d septic wounds. It is common to find plants (with apparently bisexual flowers) that do not bear fruit. The light-...own wood is hard, compact, even, elastic and very durable – so much so that it was one of the woods sought out ... early settlers for making survey pegs.

**...ature Notes:** The tiny flowers are believed to be pollinated by moths. Between September and December, these ...n produce a heavy flow of nectar, from which introduced bees produce a good, medium amber, mild-flavoured ...ney. In October, the fruit is eaten by korimako (bellbirds) and weka. And when kākāpō were on Stewart Island, ...eds were found there, year round, in their droppings. Conspicuous insects on the plant include the bright green ...ugdale's cicada' (*Kikihia dugdalei* – apparently present in the North Island only – see photo on page 46), and ...tive caterpillars of a specialist 'mingimingi leaf-tyer' moth (*Holocola parthenia*, below), which web the elongating ...w shoots together to feed on the new growth within.

**...owing It:** Seldom seen in gardens, but well suited as an ornamental shrub because of its prolific and attractive ...it. Withstands cold conditions; in cultivation it appears to prefer a light soil and fairly sunny location. Tends to ...ow to about shoulder height, but can be pruned if necessary. Usually grown from seed; striking from cuttings is ...ore difficult.

...eviously included in *Cyathodes*.

# Maukoro
# New Zealand Broom

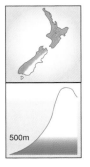

*Carmichaelia australis* [Family: Fabaceae]

| | |
|---|---|
| **Leaves:** | 5–6 mm long, usually 5–7 in a group, but *often leafless* |
| **Flowers:** | White with purple veins; tiny |
| **Seeds:** | Orange-red, *hanging in the frame-like remains of pods* 8–10 mm long (present most of the year) |
| **Other:** | *Branchlets green and strap-like (like leaves), 6–7 mm wide* |

Seeds fall to leave miniature 'nooses' on the plant – a distinctive feature that apparently inspired the Māori name ('mau' meaning 'remaining'; 'koro' meaning 'noose'). As with most New Zealand native brooms, mature plants are leafless (or nearly so); instead, very odd-looking, flattened, green branches perform the function of leaves. Many of the 40 or so native species and varieties are popular as ornamental garden plants, a fact that proved important for one, *Carmichaelia juncea*, which, until 1982, was believed to be extinct. In that year, a New Zealand botanist visiting the Royal Botanic Gardens in Edinburgh, Scotland, stumbled upon the sole surviving specimen, that had been planted there.

**Nature Notes:** Flowers pollinated primarily by native bees. Leaves eaten by kererū. Conspicuous insects include caterpillars of a native leaf-tyer moth; looper caterpillars of the 'green broom pug' (top left) and 'broom flash' (top centre); tiny caterpillars of a 'broom leafminer moth' (that make blotch mines in stems); the 'kākā beak leafminer' fly (whose tiny maggots tunnel inside stems) and the 'lemon tree borer' (wood-boring grubs of a native longhorn beetle). The shrub also supports eight specialist 'native broom weevils' (one whose grubs feed in the seedpods, three in flowerbuds, two in stem mines, one in dead wood, and one under dead bark); a 'native broom aphid'; a 'native broom gall midge'; and two 'native broom mites' (including a 'native broom gall mite' that causes 'witches' broom' and 25 mm bud galls). The twigs of more southern species are chewed for juice by kākāpō. Popular with goats. Like other members of the pea family, native brooms carry nitrogen-fixing root nodules, which help build fertility in the eroded soils of scrubland and forest edges where they tend to grow.

**Growing It:** The more showy native brooms are grown for their pretty, pea-like flowers. All are hardy, tolerating cold and practically any well-drained soil. Seeds can take a year or more to germinate unless their hard coating is first chipped or softened by pouring boiling water over them. Also easy to propagate from semi-hardwood cuttings.

This species includes what was previously known as *Carmichaelia aligera* (**North Island broom**).

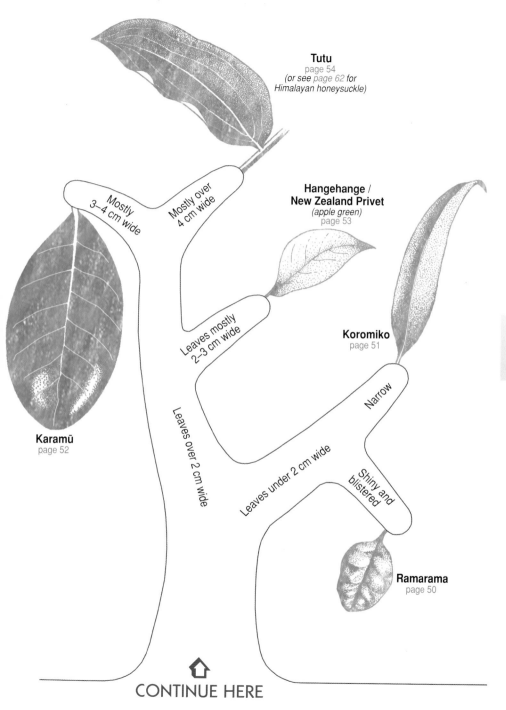

**Tutu**
page 54
*(or see page 62 for Himalayan honeysuckle)*

Mostly 3–4 cm wide

Mostly over 4 cm wide

**Hangehange / New Zealand Privet**
*(apple green)*
page 53

Leaves mostly 2–3 cm wide

**Koromiko**
page 51

**Karamū**
page 52

Leaves over 2 cm wide

Narrow

Leaves under 2 cm wide

Shiny and blistered

**Ramarama**
page 50

⬆
CONTINUE HERE

YOU CAN MEASURE THE WIDTH OF YOUR LEAF HERE

0      2    3    4 cm

# Ramarama

*Lophomyrtus bullata* [Family: Myrtaceae]

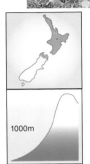

male (smaller

**Leaves:** *Blistered*, shiny, opposite, 2.5–5 cm long

**Flowers:** White, fluffy, like a miniature rātā flower (summer)

**Fruit:** Dark red to black, up to 1 cm long, on long stalks (late summer and autumn)

**Other:** A common shrub or small tree along tracksides and the edges of native forest

1000m

The blistered leaves and ripe fruit appear lacquered, making them gleam (ramarama) in the light. The wood is strong, tough, red and attractively grained, and valued by Māori for digging sticks; by pioneer bushmen for making axe handles; and by carpenters for making the handles of chisels and other such tools. In the 1950s, leafy branches fetched good prices in flower markets, where the striking foliage was used in floral arrangements to help set off brightly coloured flowers. The leaves were also an ingredient of an elaborate Māori recipe for healing bruises, and the small, ripe guava-like fruit used as food. Recent research has shown these fruit to contain *anthocyanins*, which can be effective against cancer and diabetes, the effects of aging and neurological diseases. Ramarama is also known to contain *bullatenone*, a derivative of *furfural* known to have antiseptic properties. Homespinners used the ripe berries for producing dyes.

**Nature Notes:** Honey bees collect pollen and a small amount of nectar from the flowers in summer. Fruit is eaten by kererū, tūī and korimako (bellbirds). Lichens are common on the leaves. Conspicuous insects found on the plant include at least three kinds of stick insects, including the 'large spiny stick insect' – smaller male illustrated; also several native caterpillars, including those of the 'forest semilooper' moth. The shrub also supports a 'native myrtle rootlet weevil' and is currently threatened by the arrival in 2017 of an orange-yellow rust fungus known as myrtle rust

**Growing It:** Used overseas as a conservatory plant and here as a garden shrub; planted for its eye-catching leaves and white flowers. Easy to grow in any reasonably well-drained soil, tolerating either full sun or light shade. For a bronze or reddish tint to the leaves, full sun gives best results. Generally hardy, but in the first couple of years protection from very heavy frost may be necessary. Unsuited to exposed coastal planting. Best grown from semi-hardwood cuttings taken in late summer or autumn, but can also be grown from seed.

# Koromiko

*Veronica salicifolia* and *V. stricta* (was *Hebe*) [Family: Plantaginaceae]

1000m

**Leaves:** Willow-like, 5–15 cm long, *creased along centre-line*; opposite, *each pair at right angles to the one below it*

**Flowers:** White or light blue (late summer)

**Other:** *New leaves at the growing tip are neatly pressed together.* Common on banks and tracksides

so known as **koromuka**. A 'miko' or 'muka' is a young shoot (of nīkau or coconut), linking this plant's distinctive w growth to a 'finger' ('koro', as in 'koroiti' – little finger). Such was the faith in koromiko as a cure for dysentery at it was to become the first New Zealand native plant to be listed in the 1895 edition of the British *Extra harmacopoeia*. During the Second World War, dried leaves were sent to New Zealand troops at the North African ont as a remedy for dysentery – for which they proved effective. The active ingredient was originally thought to e its tannins, but it is now known to be a *phenolic glycocide*. Other traditional Māori uses include a decoction for cers, sores, headaches, kidney and bladder troubles, sexually transmitted diseases and a catarrhal illness called itish cholera. Although koromiko produces very little wood, it was noted by early colonists for its toughness and asticity and for the fact that it gives off a lot of heat when burned.

**ature Notes:** At night, from November to early March, the flowers are visited by moths; by day by native bees, es, 'red admiral' butterflies, bellbirds and stitchbirds. Honey bees turn the nectar into a delicate light amber oney. Other conspicuous insects here include a very wide range of specialist native moth caterpillars, including ose of at least two 'Hebe plume moths' (*Platyptilia* species) top right (which bore the buds) and the 'large Hebe oper' (*Xyridacma veronicae*) (feeds on leaves). Koromiko also supports specialist 'Hebe gall midges', 'Hebe afminer flies' and 'Hebe gall mites'. On North Island koromiko (*V. stricta*), you may also find a 'Hebe mirid', a ebe seed bug' and 'Hebe psyllids'. Eaten by goats and deer, but not usually by possums.

**rowing It:** Popular for its delicate bottle-brush flowers. Hardy, growing in most situations. Can be pruned if cessary. Easily propagated from leafy cuttings. (There are more than 120 native veronicas – or hebes – nging from small trees to sprawling, cushion-like plants with whipcord branches.)

*eronica salicifolia* is mostly found in the South Island and *V. stricta* in the North Island. Otherwise, the difference between the ecies is rather technical.

**51**

# Karamū

*Coprosma lucida* and *C. robusta* [Family: Rubiaceae]

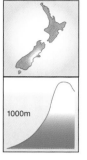

1000m

| Leaves: | *Opposite*, 5–12 cm long, with tiny bumps where the side veins join the central vein, and a bud-like scale where the leaves meet on the stem |
| --- | --- |
| Flowers: | Greenish-white, spindly, in loose clusters (spring) |
| Fruit: | Reddish-orange, 6–12 mm (most of the year) |

This and related plants are also known as **kāramuramu**, **kakaramū**, **karangū** or **kakarangū**, 'mū' or 'ngū' meaning 'speechless'; 'kakara', 'smell' or 'taste'. The Latin name, *Coprosma* (particularly *C. foetidissima*), is more explicit: 'smells of dung'. The plant's most important use to Māori seems to have been the ceremonial use of a branch by tohunga to lift illness-causing 'spells'. The fruit were sometimes eaten by Māori children but, when other food was scarce, also by adults. Medicinal uses include a decoction of the leaves to reduce fevers and for kidney trouble, an infusion of the young shoots for bladder stoppage and inflammation, and small quantities of liquid from the boiled inner bark for stomach-ache and vomiting. Māori also used the bark to produce an 'old-gold' colour for dyeing flax. Karamū belongs to the same family as coffee, a fact that inspired experiments in the late 1870s to find out whether the roasted and ground seeds might make a worthwhile substitute for that popular drink. I tried it too; the aroma *is* convincing but the seeds are small and the taste unimpressive. Large-scale production was never attempted.

**Nature Notes:** Wind pollinated. Fruit eaten at night by geckos, skinks and possums; by day by tūī, kererū, bellbirds, silvereyes (tauhou), whiteheads, stitchbirds, kiwi, weka and ship rats. Leaves by kōkako and kererū, red deer and goats but not usually by possums. Native mistletoes sometimes grow on the branches. Insects here include the native 'New Zealand vegetable bug', caterpillars of several 'Coprosma carpet' moths (both photos), a leaf-tyer and 'Coprosma leafminer moth'; also a 'karamū mirid', a 'karamū longhorn' beetle and a 'Coprosma leaf beetle' (chews holes in young leaves). Plants also support three 'Coprosma gall mites'. Leaf loss and dieback can be caused by the cabbage tree phytoplasma disease.

**Growing It:** Roots readily from cuttings, but can also be grown from seed. Can be pruned to shape and grown in a shrub border or as shelter. To get karamū to fruit, it is necessary to plant shrubs of both sexes. Hardy. A good plant for attracting birds.

The central vein on the leaf of a *Coprosma lucida* is slightly raised on the top surface; on *C. robusta* it is not.

# Hangehange
# New Zealand Privet

*Geniostoma ligustrifolium* var. *ligustrifolium* [Family: Loganiaceae]

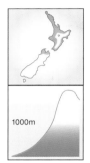

1000m

**Leaves:** *Waxy, opposite*, 4–8 cm long, *the colour of Granny Smith apples*

**Flowers:** Greenish-white, small, strong-smelling (spring)

**Fruit:** Small green seed capsules, turning black (summer)

**Other:** Looks rather like the garden privet; branches brittle

The ancestors of Māori arriving in New Zealand recognised this plant from the Austral and southern Cook Islands, giving it the same name used (in various forms) for local species of *Geniostoma*. Hangehange is the Tai Tokerau (Northland) pronunciation; known elsewhere as **whangewhange**. The leaves were bundled around lengths of dwarf cabbage tree roots (and other foods) as a form of flavouring, when such foods were being cooked in a hāngī. The sap was used medicinally – applied to areas of skin disease in children – and the bark used for scabies. Māori also collected the bark and pounded it to a pulp before soaking it in water to obtain a pure black colour for dyeing flax. Flowering signalled the fourth month of the Māori calendar (August–September). Nowadays, some websites suggest making salads from the leaves or leaf tips. While nibbling small quantities may not present a problem, it should be noted that rats fed dried leaves at 60 per cent of their rations died and many members of the same plant family are known to contain poisonous alkaloids including *strychnine*, and the potent arrow poison, *curare*.

**Nature Notes:** August to October honey bees collect a thin, pale, aromatic nectar from the strong-smelling flowers, which are also visited by native bees, hover flies and weevils, and three native honeyeater birds: tūī, bellbirds and hihi (stitchbirds). Seed capsules are eaten by kererū (New Zealand pigeons), pōpokotea (whitehead) and possibly kōkako. Caterpillars of the native 'small hook-tip looper' (*Homodotis megaspilata*) moth (top) feed on fallen leaves, while those of the native 'black-lyre leafroller' (*Cnephasia' jactatana*) moth web together dying parts of plants. In many areas, plants are threatened due to their being freely eaten by deer, goats and possums.

**Growing It:** Not generally available for sale, but attractive for its shiny, lime green leaves. A useful shrub to plant in the shade of trees, where few other plants will grow. Requires good drainage and is sensitive to heavy frost. Fast growing. Usually grown from seed but may also be grown from semi-hardwood cuttings.

# Tutu
# Tree Tutu

*Coriaria arborea* [Family: Coriariaceae]

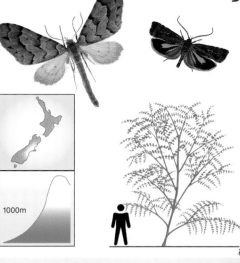

1000m

**Leaves:** Mostly opposite, *with 3–5 parallel veins*, shiny and dark on top, 5–10 cm long

**Fruit:** Swollen purple-black petals, hanging in long strings (summer and autumn)

**Other:** *Stems square-sided*. The poisonous growing shoot (in spring) looks deceptively like a large spear of asparagus

'Tutu' is the name of a look-alike fish-poison tree of the tropical Pacific, hoops of which are used as net-spreaders (tutu). Every part of the New Zealand shrub (except for the juice of the swollen purple-black petals) is likewise POISONOUS, involving convulsions, vomiting, exhaustion, coma and memory loss – even death. Yet tutu petal juice, carefully filtered through toetoe seedheads to remove the highly toxic seeds, provided Māori with an important drink, used to sweeten bracken root cakes, or made into jelly by adding seaweed. The poison (*tutin*) in the rest of the plant is so toxic that even the young succulent shoots have killed several visiting circus elephants. In dry weather, when usual sources of forest nectar give out, honey bees also collect a sweet honeydew left on the branches by the introduced 'passionvine hopper' insect (that has sucked on tutu sap). This does no harm to the bees, but this tutu honey is highly toxic to people and, in areas where tutu commonly grows, beekeepers need to take special precautions. Old tutu stems were sometimes hollowed to make Māori flutes (instead of using more traditional human bones). Tender shoots were also mashed into poultices for bruises, cuts and boils, while bark and twigs provided an excellent blue-black dye. '*Coriaria*' (from the Latin word for leather) refers to the bark being rich in tannin (16.8% in this case). Known in Northland as **tūpākihi**.

**Nature Notes:** Wind pollinated. Fruit and seeds eaten by lizards, kererū, kōkako and kākāpō. Apart from the insects just mentioned, other conspicuous species include the 'forest shield bug' (*Oncacontias vittatus*), right and several caterpillars: those of two 'tutu leafminer moths' (*Caloptilia* species, that mine leaves or fold over tips); those of three native 'leaf-tyer moths' (web leaves together); caterpillars of the 'orange flash' (*Hierodoris illita*) moth (top right) feed inside live stems; and looper caterpillars of the 'tutu green spindle' (*Tatosoma lestevata*) moth feed on leaves. Nitrogen-fixing root nodules help enrich the soil. The poisons do nothing to deter possums, which freely eat the leaves and fruit, destroying many plants.

**Growing It:** Not generally cultivated, but can be grown from a root or seed. Very hardy.

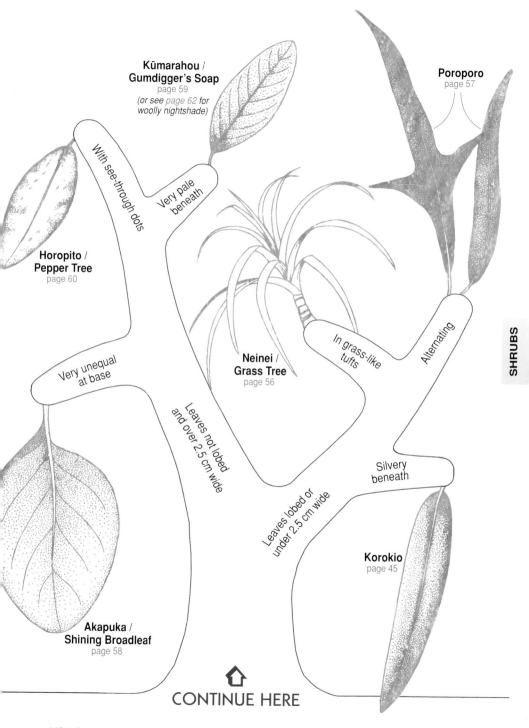

**Kūmarahou /
Gumdigger's Soap**
page 59
*(or see page 62 for
woolly nightshade)*

**Poroporo**
page 57

With see-through dots

Very pale
beneath

**Horopito /
Pepper Tree**
page 60

Very unequal
at base

**Neinei /
Grass Tree**
page 56

In grass-like
tufts

Alternating

**SHRUBS**

Leaves not lobed
and over 2.5 cm wide

Silvery
beneath

Leaves lobed or
under 2.5 cm wide

**Korokio**
page 45

**Akapuka /
Shining Broadleaf**
page 58

⌂
CONTINUE HERE

YOU CAN MEASURE THE WIDTH OF YOUR LEAF HERE ├── 2.5 cm ──┤

# Neinei
# Grass Tree

*Dracophyllum latifolium* [Family: Ericaceae]

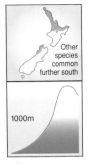

Other species common further south

1000m

| | |
|---|---|
| **Leaves:** | *Grass-like*, 25–60 cm long by 2.5–4 cm wide, shiny on top, arching in tufts at the ends of branches |
| **Other:** | Has a tropical look, rather similar to a cabbage tree. Very noticeable leaf scars remain along the trunk. Fallen leaves decay slowly on the forest floor |

An alternative Māori name, **emiemi**, means 'gathered together'. The name 'neinei' (which means 'reaching out') is shared by a Rarotongan tree (*Fitchia speciosa*) whose leaves are also clustered together, falling to leave ring-like scars on the stems. The tuft-like mop of leaves of the New Zealand tree has similarly been likened to those of the truffula trees of Dr Seuss's famous children's book, *The Lorax*. Though spindly-trunked, its timber was recommended in the late nineteenth century for inlaying in marquetry-type work; it is white, veined with red.

These channelled stems were also valued by Māori as walking sticks and for making flutes and the leaves woven by northern tribes into fine-quality clothes. In Fiordland, archaeological digs have turned up evidence that leaves of more southern species were similarly woven. The reddish leaf colouring is due to *anthocyanins* which absorb green light and which may give the plant some protection against strong sunlight. Also known as **spiderwood** or **needle-leaved neinei**. New Zealand has many native species, all with narrow, strap-like or bristly leaves. Well-known species include the much narrower-leaved **inanga** or **turpentine scrub** (so called because it ignites easily) and the exotic-looking **mountain neinei** or **pineapple tree** (named for the similarity of its leaf tufts to those of pineapple).

**Nature Notes:** *Dracophyllum* species are generally pollinated at night by moths. When kākāpō were on Little Barrier Island, the shoots and leaves proved to be a favourite food. Conspicuous insects on the plant include the 'spiny ridge-backed stick insect'. Other insects found here include tiny caterpillars of two species of 'Dracophyllum leafminer moths' (*Stigmella* species, chewing tunnels inside the leaves); grubs of two 'neinei weevils' (in dying stalks); a 'Dracophyllum mealybug'; and a 'Dracophyllum scale'. Rarer, but of special interest are the fat, pink caterpillars of the 'great tawny snoutlet' moth (*Glaphyrarcha euthrepta*) which live at the base of the leaves.

**Growing It:** Planted for its remarkable foliage. This species is one of the easier grass trees to grow, standing practically any type of soil and – once established – tolerant of fairly dry conditions. Prefers some shade. Propagated by seed or from cuttings. Grows slowly.

# Poroporo

*Solanum aviculare* [Family: Solanaceae]

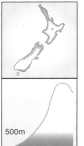

500m

**SHRUBS**

| | |
|---|---|
| **Leaves:** | Alternating, mostly lance-shaped or lobed, 10–30 cm long, dark, soft |
| **Flowers:** | White to *blue-purple*, 2–2.5 cm across (throughout most of the year) |
| **Fruit:** | *Yellow to orange*, 2.5 cm long (throughout most of the year) |
| **Other:** | Most common along the edges of forest and in scrub |

oroporo is a Pacific-wide Polynesian term for *Solanum* (nightshade) plants. The fruits of the local poroporo taste e something between a sweet date and a tomato and were an important food of Māori but they must be fully IPE, just before the skins start to burst. In the Wellington area, Europeans collected them for making jams and es. Unripe, the acrid POISONS (*solasonine* and *solamargine*) burn the throat. In severe cases, eating green erries or leaves can cause abdominal pain, vomiting, diarrhoea and depression. Homespinners used leaves and vigs to produce greenish dyes. Māori hollowed out stems to make traditional flutes, using all parts as a treatment r scabies and as a healing salve. This is consistent with Polish findings that its antibiotic constituents control hair seases in guinea pigs and rabbits, ringworm in chinchillas and skin disease in cattle. Up until 1981, the shrub was rown in Taranaki for the manufacture of hormonal steroids for birth control and the relief of rheumatoid arthritis. rom here, it was introduced to the former Soviet Union, where a postage stamp depicting the plant was issued in 972. From Russia it was exported to India. The seeds are believed to have been originally brought to New ealand by birds from Australia, where the plant is known as **kangaroo apple** (from the leaf shape being likened to kangaroo's footprint). Juice from the leaves was used for sizing wood in preparation for applying ochre as paint.

**ature Notes:** The flowers are buzz-pollinated by native hover flies, bristle flies and native bees. Fruit eaten by tūī, ellbirds, kererū, pūkeko, kākā, kākāriki (parakeets), kākāpō and silvereyes (tauhou). Other conspicuous insects ere include two introduced 'shield bugs' (the 'green potato bug' and 'green vegetable bug', *Nezara viridula*) and aterpillars of several moths, including the 'silver Y moth' (*Chrysodeixis eriosoma*) and two introduced moths (the otato moth' and 'tomato stem borer'). The plant also supports two specialists: caterpillars of the 'poroporo fruit rer' moth (*Sceliodes cordalis*) and a 'poroporo gall mite', which distorts the leaves and damages shoots.

**rowing It:** Planted for its bright flowers and bird-attracting fruit. Easy to propagate by cuttings or from seed. lowers best in full sun. Prefers a well-drained soil. Very quick growing.

**57**

# Akapuka
# Shining Broadleaf

*Griselinia lucida* [Family: Griseliniaceae]

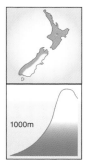

1000m

**Leaves:** *Mature leaves very unequal-sided at the base, very glossy, alternating, 7–17 cm long. (Leaves of* **kāpuka**, *Griselinia littoralis, are only slightly uneven at the base)*

**Fruit:** Dark purple, 8 mm long (summer, autumn and winter)

**Other:** Often grows up in trees, where furrowed grooves on the thick stem are distinctive

Although akapuka (or **puka**) will grow directly on the forest floor, it thrives best up in trees, often starting life in the midst of a perching lily high in a mature rimu or kahikatea, where it has full access to the light. Even up here, it can be picked out from the surrounding foliage by its unusually glossy, light-coloured leaves and by its deeply furrowed, vine-like aerial roots. These roots grow toward the ground at the rate of over one metre per year to eventually establish the plant as a vine that can swing free of its support. The leaves and root hairs are especially adapted to optimise the absorption of rain and reduce evaporation. The small amount of wood the plant produces is light brown, dense, compact and durable. In pioneer days it was used for fence posts, for building and repairing mills. 'Puka' is a name from the tropical Polynesian homeland, referring to two large-leaved trees. In New Zealand, the name is frequently used also for an unrelated, large-leaved tree, *Meryta sinclairii* (naturally found only on the Three Kings Islands and on the Hen and Chicken Islands but now quite widely grown in northern gardens). The Māori names for *Griselinia lucida*, akapuka and **akakōpuka**, make the distinction clear, since 'aka' means 'vine'.

**Nature Notes:** In September and October, bees collect a dull yellow pollen and occasionally some nectar from the many small, green or yellow flowers. Kererū (New Zealand pigeons) – and possibly also kōkako – eat the fruit. Where goats and deer can reach the plant, it is freely eaten by them. The tree also supports a 'Griselinia leafminer weevil' (*Peristoreus discoideus*) whose tiny grubs make large blotch mines in the leaves.

**Growing It:** Planted for its large, bright, exceptionally glossy leaves, as a hedge plant, as a specimen shrub in the open or in a large container. Often grown from seed but can also be grown from semi-hardwood cuttings, though these can be difficult to root. Useful in coastal gardens since it will withstand cold conditions, salt winds and poor sandy soil. Easy to grow in direct sun or light shade and tolerates most soil types.

# Kūmarahou
# Gumdigger's Soap

*Pomaderris kumeraho* [Family: Rhamnaceae]

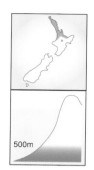

500m

**Leaves:** *Blue-green on top; underside pale with protruding veins*; alternating, 5–8 cm long

**Flowers:** Creamy yellow, fragrant, in large, fluffy clusters (early spring)

**Other:** Whole plant covered in a soft mat of hair. Found along forest edges (especially kauri forest), common on poor clay hills and along roadsides

The Māori name refers to this shrub flowering in the latter half of September – a good indicator of when to plant kūmara – 'hou' meaning both 'new' and 'to force downwards'. The plant's common European name refers to the fact that the flowers – and to a lesser extent the broken leaves – can be rubbed between wet hands to produce a thick and very effective lather. When digging for gum, workers used this for washing – something I have also done when my own hands were thickly covered in grease from a roadside engine repair job; it proved remarkably effective. This detergent property is due to appreciable amounts of *saponins* (soap-like chemicals) in the plant, which chemists suggest could be biotransformed to precursors for steroid hormones. Kūmarahou was, and still is, widely used in Northland for relief of all chest complaints and as a 'blood purifier' and is one of the few New Zealand native plants to have turned up in English herbals. The leaves are generally boiled and the liquid drunk; this tastes exceedingly bitter but has a curiously sweet aftertaste. The leaves and flowers have been shown to contain the *flavonols*, *quercetin* and *kaempferol* and the *dicoumarin ellagic acid* (which controls bleeding) and its *O-methyl ethers*, some of which may account for its reputed medicinal properties.

**Nature Notes:** The flowers produce a dark, strongly flavoured nectar and creamy-white pollen that is collected by bees. Conspicuous native insects found on the plant include the native 'New Zealand vegetable bug' (*Glaucias myoti*) which sucks the sap (as opposed to the introduced green vegetable bug on page 57) and caterpillars of the 'sharp-tipped bell moth' (*Epalxiphora axenana*) which web leaves together. Attractive roadside plants are frequently destroyed by road maintenance workers.

**Growing It:** Planted for its grand show of yellow spring flowers which it produces at an early age. Prefers sun and well-drained soil. Sensitive to frost. Easily grown from seed.

# Horopito
# Pepper Tree

*Pseudowintera axillaris* and *P. colorata* [Family: Winteraceae]

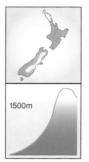

1500m

| | |
|---|---|
| **Leaves:** | Alternating, with see-through dots, *strong-smelling when crushed, peppery to taste* (unlike karapapa) |
| **Flowers:** | Greenish-yellow (spring) |
| **Fruit:** | Orange-red (on *P. axillaris*) to black (summer and autumn) |
| **Other:** | Bark almost black. (The **mountain horopito**, *P. colorata*, often has larger red blotches on its leaves) |

The Māori name implies a 'forest edge' species, for 'horo' means 'landslip'; and 'pito', 'at first'. An alternative name, **puhikawa**, hints at the plant's tapu nature (puhi), describing the peppery taste of the leaves ('kawa' meaning 'unpleasant tasting, sour or bitter'). An old European name, **Māori painkiller**, likewise refers to the leaves being chewed to alleviate toothache and diarrhoea. European settlers used the bark as a substitute for quinine (a painkiller that reduces fevers). The leaves have recently become popular in some restaurants as an indigenous spice. Twenty-nine components of its essential oil have so far been identified, including a dental analgesic called *eugenol*. Another interesting find is a compound called *polygodial*, which acts as an antibiotic, especially against the yeast *Candida albicans*, which can cause thrush in infants, and skin infections. *Anthocyanins* in the leaves (the plant's equivalent of sunburn cream) account for their red tint. The wood seldom amounts to much and lacks durability, but was occasionally used for its highly ornamental effect (reddish with paler markings) as a veneer.

**Nature Notes:** Flowers pollinated by small flies, beetles, thrips, and by looper caterpillars 'Tarzaning' on silk threads from tree to tree. Fruit eaten by kererū and ship rats. Conspicuous insects here include tree wētā and three looper caterpillars ('horopito flash' (*Pseudocoremia fascialata*), 'forest semilooper' and 'kawakawa looper') and five 'leaf-tyer' moth caterpillars (including a 'horopito leaf-tyer'), and those of a 'horopito shoot-borer'. Horopito also supports two species of 'horopito whitefly' and grubs of two 'horopito weevils' (one in fruit; one in dead wood). The *terpene* content of the leaves (9% by weight) deters browsing possums, deer and goats, allowing it to become a fairly dominant shrub in North Island beech forest.

**Growing It:** Easy to grow in most soils. Tolerates cold. Propagated by seed or cuttings. *Pseudowintera colorata* is often preferred because of its more colourful foliage.

Properties refer primarily to the **lowland horopito**, *Pseudowintera axillaris*, but many apply also to the more shrubby **mountain horopito**. Rather confusingly, the name **pepper tree** has also sometimes been used for kawakawa (*Macropiper excelsum*) – see *Which Native Tree?*

# Conspicuous Flowers and Berries

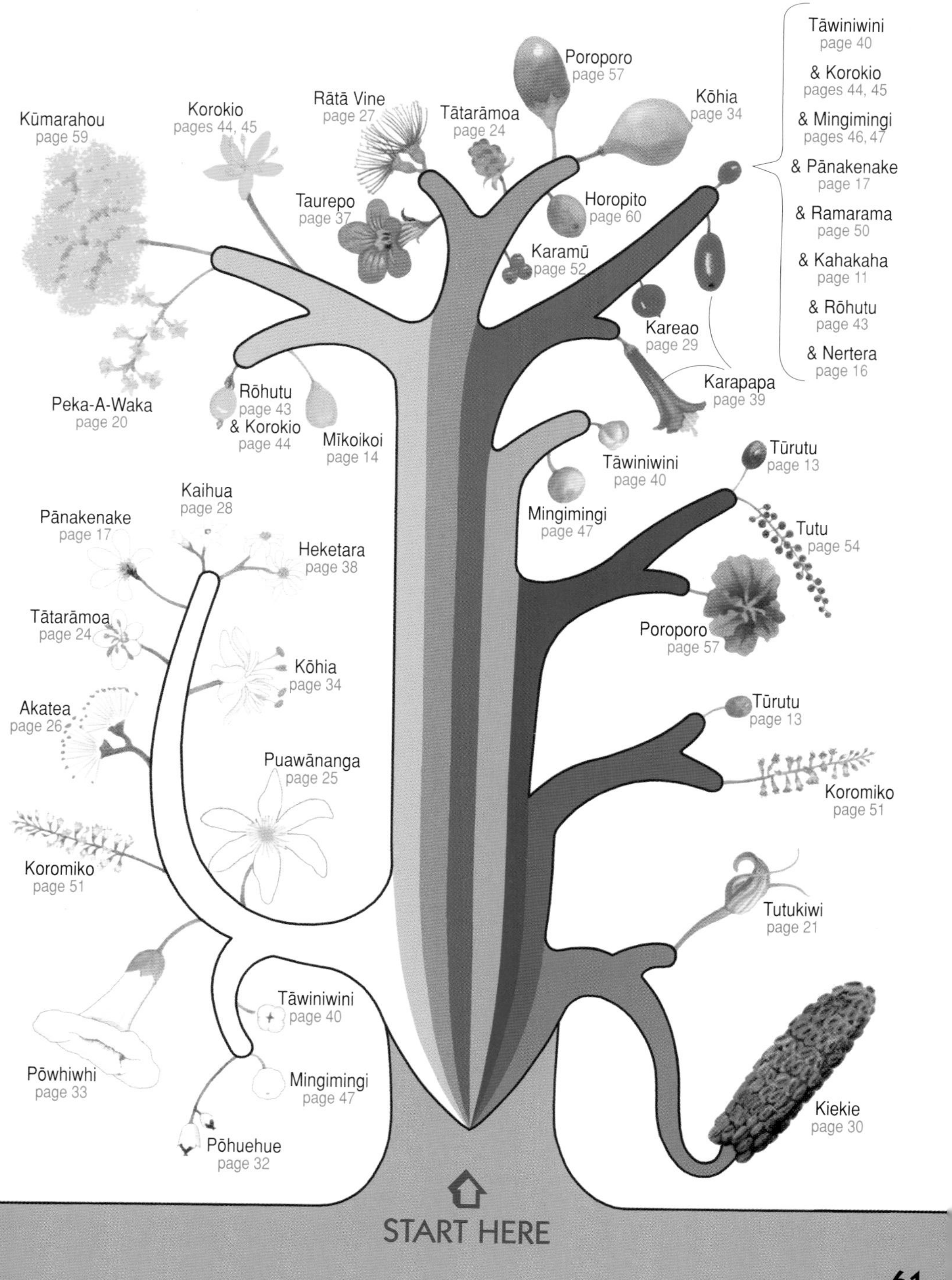

Tāwiniwini
page 40

& Korokio
pages 44, 45

& Mingimingi
pages 46, 47

& Pānakenake
page 17

& Ramarama
page 50

& Kahakaha
page 11

& Rōhutu
page 43

& Nertera
page 16

Poroporo
page 57

Kōhia
page 34

Kūmarahou
page 59

Korokio
pages 44, 45

Rātā Vine
page 27

Tātarāmoa
page 24

Taurepo
page 37

Horopito
page 60

Karamū
page 52

Kareao
page 29

Karapapa
page 39

Rōhutu
page 43
& Korokio
page 44

Mīkoikoi
page 14

Peka-A-Waka
page 20

Kaihua
page 28

Tāwiniwini
page 40

Tūrutu
page 13

Pānakenake
page 17

Heketara
page 38

Mingimingi
page 47

Tutu
page 54

Tātarāmoa
page 24

Kōhia
page 34

Poroporo
page 57

Akatea
page 26

Puawānanga
page 25

Tūrutu
page 13

Koromiko
page 51

Koromiko
page 51

Tutukiwi
page 21

Tāwiniwini
page 40

Pōwhiwhi
page 33

Mingimingi
page 47

Kiekie
page 30

Pōhuehue
page 32

⌂
START HERE

61

# Troubleshooting

## Is it a shrub or a tree?

Generally speaking, if it has a distinct woody trunk, it is a tree. Trees are covered in the companion volume, **Which Native Tree?** The distinction, however, is not always simple; some plants can be shrubs and trees. Kawakawa and mānuka, for example, can be either. Although you will find them in the tree book, for convenience, photos of them are repeated here. Two common native trees (kaikōmako and putaputāwētā) are particularly tricky in that they have very different shrub-like forms when young, so images of the juvenile forms of these are likewise repeated here:

kawakawa                 mānuka                 kaikōmako                 putaputāwētā

## Is it a fern?

If you think the plant you have found may be a fern, take a look at the growing shoot and the back of the leaves. If the growing shoot is coiled like the head of a violin, or if the backs of some leaves are covered with raised brown patches or lines, it is most likely a fern. Ferns are covered in the companion volume, **Which Native Fern?**

## Is it native?

Several foreign plants now grow wild in native forest; some of these are quite widespread. Eight of the most common and striking examples are illustrated here:

banana passionfruit      blackberry             Himalayan honeysuckle      old man's beard

sycamore                 wandering Jew          wild ginger                woolly nightshade

# Selected References

Aston, B.C. 'The Indigenous Tans and Vegetable Dyestuffs of New Zealand.' Parts I and II. *N. Z. J. Agriculture* 15: 55–62, 1917; 15: 117–28, 1917 and 16: 358–65, 1918.

Beever, James. *A Dictionary of Maori Plant Names.* Auckland Botanical Society, 1987.

Best, Elsdon. 'Food Products of Tuhoeland.' *Trans. N. Z. Inst.* 35: 45–111, 1902.

Best, Elsdon. *Forest Lore of the Maori.* Government Printer, 1942.

Bishop, Nic. *Natural History of New Zealand.* Hodder and Stoughton, 1992.

Bloor, Stephen. 'A survey of extracts of New Zealand indigenous plants for selected biological activities.' *N. Z. J. Botany*, 33: 523–540, 1995.

Brockie, Robert. *A Living New Zealand Forest.* Bateman, 1992.

Brooker, S. G., Cambie, R. C. and Cooper, R. C. *New Zealand Medicinal Plants.* Heinemann, 1987.

Colenso, William. 'On the Botany of the North Island of New Zealand.' *Trans. N. Z. Inst.* 1: 1–58, 1868. (In part 3 – essays.)

Colenso, William. 'On the Māori Races of New Zealand.' *Trans. N. Z. Inst.* 1: 1–58, 1868. (In part 3 – essays.)

Connor, H. E. *The Poisonous Plants in New Zealand.* Government Printer, 1977.

Cooper, R. C. and Cambie, R. C. *New Zealand's Economic Native Plants.* Oxford University Press, 1991.

Crowe, Andrew. *A Field Guide to the Native Edible Plants of New Zealand.* Penguin, 2004.

Dawson, John. *Forest Vines to Snow Tussocks: The Story of New Zealand Plants.* Victoria University Press, 1993.

Dawson, John & Lucas, Rob. *Nature Guide to the New Zealand Forest.* Random House (Godwit), 2000.

Fisher, Muriel E., Satchell, E. and Watkins, Janet M. *Gardening With New Zealand Plants, Shrubs and Trees.* Collins, 1970.

Fisher, Muriel and Power, Elaine. *A Touch of Nature.* Collins, 1980.

Hutchinson, Amy. *Plant Dyeing.* The Daily Telegraph Company (Napier), 1941.

King, Carolyn M. (Ed.) *The Handbook of New Zealand Mammals.* Oxford University Press, 2005.

Kirk, T. 'Notes on the Economic Properties of certain Native Grasses.' *Trans. N. Z. Inst.* 9: 494–502, 1876.

Kirk, T. *The Forest Flora of New Zealand.* Government Printer, 1889.

Lloyd, Joyce. *Dyes from Plants of Australia and New Zealand.* Reed, 1981.

Maloy, Andrew. *Plants for Free! – A New Zealand Guide to Plant Propagation.* Shoal Bay Press (Christchurch), 1992.

Matthews, Julian. *New Zealand Native Plants for Your Garden.* Pacific Publishers, 1987.

Maysmor, Bob. *Te Manu Tukutuku: a Study of the Maori Kite.* Allen & Unwin NZ, 1990.

Metcalf, L. J. *The Cultivation of New Zealand Trees and Shrubs.* Reed Methuen, 1987.

Metcalf, L. J. *The Cultivation of New Zealand Plants.* Godwit Press, 1993.

Moore, L. B. and Irwin, J. B. *The Oxford Book of New Zealand Plants.* Oxford University Press, 1987.

Mortimer, John and Bunny. *Trees for the New Zealand Countryside.* Butterworths, 1987.

Pendergrast, Mick. *Feathers and Fibre.* Penguin, 1984.

Poole, Lindsay and Adams, Nancy. *Trees and Shrubs of New Zealand.* DSIR Publishing, 1990.

Richards, E. C. *Our New Zealand Trees and Flowers.* Simpson and Williams (Christchurch), 1956.

Riley, Murdoch. *Māori Healing and Herbal.* Viking Sevenseas, 1994.

Smith-Dodsworth, John. *New Zealand Native Shrubs and Climbers.* Bateman, 1991.

*Te Ara: The Encyclopedia of New Zealand.* **http://www.teara.govt.nz/TheBush**

Walsh, R. S. *Nectar and Pollen Sources of New Zealand.* National Beekeepers' Association of New Zealand, 1978.

Williams, Herbert W. *A Dictionary of the Māori Language.* Government Printer, Wellington, 1985.

Sources for ecological information include various specialist journals: *Annals of Botany* (Oxford), *New Zealand Journal of Botany, New Zealand Journal of Zoology, New Zealand Journal of Ecology, Transactions and Proceedings of the Royal Society of New Zealand, Notornis, Tuatara, Forest and Bird, DoC Threatened Species Recovery Plans* and the Crop & Food Research invertebrate herbivore–host plant association database: **http://plant-synz.landcareresearch.co.nz**. Additional plant–animal interactions were found in photographic form through the Nga Manu Sanctuary website **http://ngamanuimages.org.nz**

For more detail on the origins of Māori names, see *Which Native Tree?* and a larger referenced project, entitled *Pathway of the Birds: The Voyaging Achievements of Māori and their Polynesian Ancestors* (Bateman, 2018).

# Index (**bold type** indicates main entries)